T0162866

enjoy!

101 Little Ways to Add FUN to Your WORK Every Day

enjoy!

Gini Graham Scott, Ph.D.

AN AUTHORS GUILD BACKINPRINT.COM EDITION

ASJA PRESS
BLOOMINGTON

ENJOY!
101 Little Ways to Add FUN to Your WORK Every Day

Copyright © 2008, 2011 by Gini Graham Scott, Ph.D.

All rights reserved. No part of this book may be used or reproduced by any means,
graphic, electronic, or mechanical, including photocopying, recording, taping or by any
information storage retrieval system without the written permission of the publisher
except in the case of brief quotations embodied in critical articles and reviews.

The views expressed in this work are solely those of the author and do not necessarily reflect the views
of the publisher, and the publisher hereby disclaims any responsibility for them.

iUniverse books may be ordered through booksellers or by contacting:

iUniverse
1663 Liberty Drive
Bloomington, IN 47403
www.iuniverse.com
1-800-Authors (1-800-288-4677)

Because of the dynamic nature of the Internet, any Web addresses or links contained in this book
may have changed since publication and may no longer be valid.

Any people depicted in stock imagery provided by Thinkstock are models,
and such images are being used for illustrative purposes only.

Certain stock imagery © Thinkstock.

ISBN: 978-1-4502-9135-4 (sc)

Printed in the United States of America

iUniverse rev. date: 1/19/2011

Contents

Introduction

ENJOY! 101 Little Ways to Add Fun to Your Work Every Day offers an antidote to today's fast-paced competitive society, where people work too hard, particularly in the United States. Compared to other industrialized countries, we work longer hours each week, take less vacation time, and have a higher level of work-related stress. Even kids in school are put on the fast track to success early on, leading to a high level of stress. And today, an ever-growing mountain of business success and professional/personal development books offers tools and techniques to help readers achieve even more.

I have become especially aware of the problem, since I specialize in improving business relationships, professional and personal development, and popular culture. Besides realizing that I was working too hard myself, I talked to dozens of people who described their barriers to enjoyment and expressed the hope of finding ways to enjoy work more.

ENJOY! describes how to identify such barriers, reduce the time spent on less enjoyable activities, enjoy whatever you are doing more, and put more enjoyable activities into your work life. Besides examples from workshops and interviews with individuals and experts, such as psychologists and recreation professionals, it features games I have developed for this book. All told, there are more than 101 different ways you can up your fun quotient to your work or workplace, while succeeding at whatever you want to do.

The book covers these main topics and includes a variety of gamcs, exercises, and tips to help you along the way. It is divided into four Parts, which include the following chapters:

Part I. Don't Worry, Be Happy

Chapter 1. The Principles of Happiness

As happiness researchers are discovering, having a happy, positive outlook can help make anything you do more enjoyable. This chapter features the results of happiness research and shows how you can mobilize those ideas to enjoy your work more.

Chapter 2. Six Tools to Help You Be Even Happier

What if you have a negative attitude causing you stress and tension? Or what if you feel angry, frustrated, bored, or in a rut due to events or circumstances? This chapter features tools and techniques to turn that negative attitude around and help you stay in the present to enjoy whatever you are doing more.

Chapter 3. What Makes People Happy?

After years of research and hundreds of research studies, psychologists and others studying what brings satisfaction and happiness to people have come up with findings about what makes people happy. This chapter lists sixty-four simple secrets to increasing your happiness in work and everyday life.

Part II. Breaking Down the Barriers to Enjoyment

Chapter 4. Assessing Where You Are

A first step to increasing your enjoyment is discovering where you are now and checking in periodically to see how you have progressed. This chapter provides techniques for examining the level of enjoyment you are experiencing now and tracking that on a daily or weekly basis.

Chapter 5. Silencing Your Inner Critical Voice

For many people, the big barrier to fully enjoying what you are doing is the inner critical voice, which has messages like: "work harder," "don't waste time," "do what everyone else is doing," and "do what your parents enjoy." So you may spend a lot of time doing what you don't want to do and don't need to do. This chapter features techniques to help you quiet and quell that inner critic.

Chapter 6. Rediscover Your Inner Child

Rediscovering your inner kid can help you both enjoy more and become more creative as you rediscover the playfulness, sponta-neity, enthusiasm, and curiosity of kids that are often lost for adults urged to exercise reason, control, and conform. This chapter focuses ways to bring out these inner kid qualities to bring more vitality into your work and life.

Chapter 7. Eliminating Other Enjoyment Blocks

You may find still other blocks to enjoyment, because of your personal experiences, such as feeling a high level of stress, being out of touch with your feelings, or being apt to worry or think about other things, so you are not fully present to enjoy what you are doing. This chapter features techniques to find and get rid of these other enjoyment blocks,

Part III. 101 Ways to Enjoy Yourself More At Work

Chapter 8. Adding More Fun to the Workplace

Even if you have to do something you don't want to do, like that pesky boring job, you can still up your enjoyment with games and other techniques to make the process more interesting and fun and get rid of any feelings of tension and anxiety. This chapter features twenty-seven ways to make whatever you have to do more fun.

Chapter 9. Make Work More Fun for Everybody

Besides adding fun to the workplace on your own—or mostly on your own—there are ways to make having fun a group activity for your department or division or for the whole office. The focus here is on thirty-one fun activities that you can introduce to others you work with in your own office—and potentially, these ideas can spread throughout a larger company, too.

Chapter 10. Organizing Events, Celebrations, and Contests

The first two chapters of Part III have given you ideas for enjoying yourself more at work making the workplace more fun for yourself and others. This chapter takes it to the next level with thirty-four ideas for organizing events, celebrations, and contests that everybody can enjoy.

Chapter 11. Take Your Fun Outside of Work

Not all fun activities with your co-workers have to take place in the workplace. Besides having fun at the office, you all can have some truly fun times off-site. This final chapter of Part III gives you nine ideas on taking your fun outside.

Part IV. Expand Your Fun Horizons

Chapter 12. Exploring New Possibilities

Trying out new activities can add spice to your life, which can make you feel better about your work, too. This chapter describes playful ways to find new possibilities, assess them, decide which ones are best for you, and try them out mentally, as well as in reality.

Chapter 13. Make Travel Time More Interesting and Enjoyable

Whether you're commuting to work or traveling for business, you can use various techniques to make your travel time more interesting. These are techniques to use when you're not already doing work along the way, say on your laptop or in a notebook, and most of them are suited to when you're traveling on a bus or train or as a passenger in a car—not when you are driving.

Chapter 14. Start an *ENJOY!* Group to Increase Your Fun with Others

Earlier chapters have focused on ways to increase your enjoyment with techniques you use on your own or by taking the initiative in suggesting activities for your co-workers to do at work. But beyond these activities, you can join with others in a more systematic way to apply these techniques. This way you both have a support group and a group to help you continually come up with creative and fun ideas to add more enjoyment to everyone's life.

Chapter 15. Putting It All Together

This chapter sums up the major strategies for having more fun in your life. There's a "What's Your Enjoyment Quotient?" Test in the back of the book for you to take before and after reading the book to assess your Enjoyment Quotient when you start the book and afterwards to assess how much more enjoyment you have added to your work and your workplace. In addition, you'll find tips on setting up your own Enjoy It More Groups to work through these chapters and apply the techniques with others. Finally, you'll see a bibliography featuring the books I used in writing *ENJOY!*—some of which you may want to read yourself.

PART I

Don't Worry, Be Happy

1

The Principles of Happiness

A good way to start enjoying your work more is to apply the principles of how to be happy that have been developed through the new science of positive psychology. Some of these principles may seem obvious once they are outlined, though researchers are now doing studies that determine how and when people feel happier. And other psychologists are identifying and applying these principles in their clinical practice, using them to relieve patients suffering from anxiety, depression, and other symptoms.

Understanding the Science of Happiness

According to psychologist Dan Baker, Director of the Life Enhancement Program at Canyon Ranch in California, "Happiness is a way of life—an overriding outlook composed of qualities such as optimism, courage, love, and fulfillment," so you enjoy every day, no matter what happens.[1] In his view, the biggest enemy of being happy is the fear system, a biologically based response derived from our lower brain, which we share with reptiles (hence our "reptilian brain"). The fear system initially developed as a survival mechanism to enable us to respond quickly at the first sign of threat, so it is triggered more quickly than our rational thoughts, our feelings of love, or any other human reactions. The more slow-acting neocortex is the source of our creative, intuitive, intellectual, and spiritual responses— and the physical site of our feelings of happiness.[2] Thus, to be truly happy, you have to overcome these fears and tap into the powers of the neocortex that make you feel happy, whether at work or in your personal life. Or as Baker explains, you need to learn how to help your neocortical brain functions—your higher thought and spirit—"dominate the lower brain functions that are focused solely upon survival."[3]

These fears can take various forms, including anger, perfectionism, pessimism, anxiety, depression,[4] and feelings of isolation, but whatever form they take, you need to overcome them by employing the qualities that make you feel happy, using specific tools to access these qualities. According to Baker, there are twelve qualities of happiness, which he identifies as: love, optimism, courage, a sense of freedom, proactivity, security, health, spirituality, altruism, perspective, humor, and purpose. As he describes it, *love* is the "wellspring of happiness," which he considers the polar opposite of fear, both emotionally and neurologically, and it is both everlasting and can be continually renewed. So in its many forms, from appreciation to love of work, friends, and significant others, love is an important quality to cultivate.[5]

You also want to be *optimistic,* so you can put painful events behind you, such as by learning from whatever difficulties you encounter. Optimism can also help you overcome any regrets for the past and lead you to feel confident about whatever the future will bring.

Courage is important as a way to overcome feelings of fear, and *freedom* represents your power of choice, which you can always exercise whatever the situation. You just need the courage to use that power, according to Baker.

Being *proactive* is another key because it enables you to shape your own destiny, rather than waiting for other people or events to make you happy. *Security* involves liking and accepting who you are, so you have an inner sense of assurance, since everything else in life changes. Security has to come from within, not from outer attributes, such as money or popularity.

Being in good *health* is important, too, because you need to feel healthy to be happy—and at the same time, feeling happy will contribute to your good health.

Spirituality doesn't mean you have a particular religious faith, but rather that you are open to experiences beyond your everyday life.

Altruism brings great satisfaction through giving to others and feeling connected to them; it helps provide you with a sense of purpose. By contrast, people who are not altruistic tend to be too self-absorbed to be truly happy.

Perspective is important for making distinctions, such as between big and small problems, and prioritizing what's more and less important, rather than being rigid. This view also enables you to put difficulties into a larger context, so you remain attuned to the big picture.

It also helps to look on whatever happens with a sense of *humor*. Even during bad times, humor will help you lighten up and move past those difficulties.

Finally, having a sense of *purpose* gives meaning to your life. You feel a sense of satisfaction that you are doing what you were meant to do.

Applying the Happiness Principles in Your Work

How might you apply these happiness principles in your own life, especially at work?

First, you may recognize that you are already using many of these principles in your own work or life. But now pay attention to how and when you are using them, so you appreciate yourself for what you are already doing. In fact, that's the first of the principles: love, or in this case, showing appreciation for yourself, or self-love.

You can use the following chart to help you assess what you are already doing and rate how regularly you are using that principle on a scale of 0–5. Use the last column to note your comments on what you might want to do to better put that principle into practice.

How I Am Already Applying the Happiness Principles		
Happiness Principles	Rating (from 0–5)	What I Might Do
Love		
Optimism		
Courage		
Sense of Freedom		
Proactivity		
Security		
Health		
Spirituality		
Altruism		
Perspective		
Humor		
Purpose		

Second, however much you are already applying these principles, consider how you might apply them in different situations.

Say you are feeling upset about a particular job assignment

because you feel it is too hard for you, you lack important information to do the job right, you don't like the team members assigned to work on the project with you, or whatever. Or suppose as a manager, you feel you are being overworked and pressured with too many deadlines, feel stressed because of conflicts within your department, and are underappreciated for your past accomplishments. How might you put into practice the twelve happiness principles to feel better about your situation—or change your circumstances for the better, so you feel happier about that?

1. Whatever the challenge, however difficult the situation, think about what you can appreciate about it, rather than focusing on what is wrong with it. For example, look on it as an opportunity to master new skills, such as performing the particular job, learning to better get along with team members, prioritizing what's most important so you can better organize the task, or working out ways to help people in a dispute get along.

2. Feel optimistic that you will overcome these difficulties and learn from your experience for the future.

3. Find the courage to stand up to discuss the problem, delegate some of the tasks, or say no to more responsibilities, so you feel less pressured. This courage might also help you claim the deserved recognition you feel you haven't gotten, whether you do so by sending a memo, having a discussion with the person you feel should give you the credit, or noting that you have done a certain previously unacknowledged task at a staff meeting.

4. Feel a sense of freedom by reminding yourself that you have a choice in what tasks you will do, organizing your schedule so you can better perform the tasks, or deciding whether you want to keep this job or move on to something else.

5. Then, be proactive in taking action to make the desired changes now. This way you don't just think about what might

be if you did something or someone else did something, but you take steps to change what you want to change *now*.

6. Reaffirm your feeling of security that you are the master of your own choices and actions. Remind yourself that your security doesn't depend on your financial status, because you can cut back if necessary if you need to look for a better job opportunity and that true happiness comes not from the money itself but from doing something that is satisfying to do.

7. Reflect on what's good about your health now, which will help you feel healthier, too, rather than thinking about what's wrong. For example, praise yourself for your high level of energy and alertness; give yourself kudos for the healthy foods you have been eating; recognize that you haven't had a cold or other serious illness for the past year; and so on. In short, pay homage to where you have been especially healthy, and the sense of satisfaction that comes with this process will provide healing energy to positively influence your physical, emotional, and mental health.

8. As for the spiritual dimension, think about how your own religious faith or feelings of connection to others or to some sense of purpose or meaning that has helped you feel stronger in doing whatever you are doing. For example, if you are religious, give thanks to God or Allah for being beside you, helping you feel strong, and guiding you in making the right choices for you. Or if you are not religious, feel imbued with a sense of energy or power coming from the universe or from within yourself giving you this strength and guidance, so you feel confident and assured in your actions.

9. To incorporate the principle of altruism, think about how whatever you are doing can help others. Even if your work is only a small part of a larger effort, think about how the work as a whole will be of benefit to others. This way you feel more con-

nected to the work community as a whole and feel the satisfaction that comes from helping others.

10. For perspective, consider how these difficulties are only a small part of your work or how you will be able to overcome them just as you have conquered other difficulties in the past. Or, as another possibility, imagine you are looking back several months in the future, seeing this as just a small bump on a pathway to success, or as a job that will help you move on to another job you like even more.

11. Add a touch of humor, too, by imagining yourself looking upon whatever you are experiencing as an outside observer watching yourself. That might help you see the levity or ridiculousness of what you are going through now. For instance, as you struggle with some task—whether it's paperwork or dealing with a hard-to-move physical object—you might imagine yourself viewing a comedy film in which your struggles are so exaggerated that they become hilarious to view—and you are certain to feel better about whatever you are doing as well.

12. And finally, think of whatever task you are doing, however unpleasant it might be now, as part of a larger purpose, such as to help you along your career path or to give you more insights for the future.

You don't have to use all of the principles in any given situation, but draw on those that seem most appropriate to turn whatever you are doing into a more pleasant, happier experience, whether at work or in your personal life.

That's exactly what I did in a couple of situations that came up during the time I was writing this chapter. First, I have a business I have been trying to sell through a broker unsuccessfully for about eight months. But instead of letting feelings of frustration demoralize me, I was able to transform this situation into something positive. One way was to simply accept the situation for now, appreciate it, and, as they say, "Make the best of it." Since the business has been very successful and profitable, even though I don't want to run it, I decided not to walk away from it, but make it more manageable, so I would have to spend less time running it—by grouping activities together and by hiring assistants who could handle different parts of the business. Also, I didn't let the business hold me back from moving on to other things; I took some computer equipment and office supplies with me to a satellite office in Santa Monica, so I could run the business while I conduct other business there. And in the meantime, I began a systematic search for a business broker with more experience than the first broker.

When I had to deal with a difficult client, I found a way to transform that into a more positive experience, too. In this case, the client wanted me to write up a letter for her to pitch an article about a fairly obscure historical event that occurred in a small European village. However, after I drafted her letter, she had a number of nit-picky corrections that would normally be made in a final editorial polish stage. Then after a rewrite, she said she wanted to do her own rewrite and expected a refund for writing the letter, although in fact she used most of my letter in doing her own rewrite of a few sections. My initial reaction was to feel angry and challenge her request for a refund. But as I thought about the situation, using some of the principles outlined above, I reminded myself that she was still paying several hundred dollars for sending out her pitch. And since I was doing a major database update, I could increase the prices for both her and others for sending out a query, whereas without this experience I would have left the prices at their current lower amount. So in the short term, I would be earning only a small amount less for her letter and, in the long run, I'd be able to make more for the query service for everyone. I also reminded myself that if she was taking the responsibility for writing the letter, she would not be able to blame anyone else for the results if her query for an obscure, hard-to-market article wasn't successful.

In short, I found ways to turn what were initially frustrating experiences into positive learning and growth experiences, both in dealing with my business as a whole and in dealing with individual customers. I thought in terms of appreciating what I could, making choices to improve what was possible, proactively coming up with alternatives, feeling secure that things would work out, and looking toward the future, rather than regretting and feeling upset and trapped by the past.

Putting the Principles to Work in the Here and Now

So is there some situation you are facing now where you might apply these twelve happiness principles to feel better? Or perhaps you have a friend or associate with a problem, and you'd like to help that person work through the situation using these principles. You can use the chart on the following page to help you work through the situation and apply those principles that are appropriate to that situation.

How Can I Feel Better About a Difficult Situation?

Description of the Situation:

Happiness Principles	How I Might Apply These Principles in This Situation
Love	
Optimism	
Courage	
Sense of Freedom	
Proactivity	
Security	
Health	
Spirituality	
Altruism	
Perspective	
Humor	
Purpose	

2

Six Tools to Help You Be Even Happier

The last chapter featured the key qualities of happiness. This chapter will focus on using various tools and techniques to become even happier. According to Dan Baker, there are six key tools you can use, as well as five traps to avoid.[1] After listing these briefly, I'll suggest some exercises you can use to apply these principles.

The six tools are appreciation, choice, personal power, leading with your strengths, using language and stories effectively, and multidimensional living—in other words, leading a full life. The five traps are trying to buy happiness with money, or find it through the pursuit of pleasure, by resolving the past, overcoming your weaknesses, or forcing yourself to be happy.[2] Here's how to apply each of these tools.

Showing Appreciation

Appreciation is fundamental in Baker's view, because it is a form of love that "asks for nothing and gives everything," and, in coming from the neocortex, it overcomes feelings of fear that derive from the lower, "reptilian" brain.[3] It does so because, according to scientists, the brain can't be in a state of appreciation and fear at the same time; though you might go back and forth between these states, they are mutually exclusive.[4] In fact, researchers who have studied these states have found that people who are experiencing positive emotions, having just seen a happy film, are better able to focus and solve problems than people who have just seen an upsetting film.[5] Researchers have found that there is an interaction between having positive thoughts and feelings and the brain's biochemistry. When you think and feel positively, your brain produces more dopamine, which is a key neurotransmitter linked to feelings of satisfaction, so you are further inspired to have positive thoughts and feelings, creating an upward spiral.[6] By contrast, thinking and feeling negatively can trigger a downward spiral, until something breaks the process to get you thinking and feeling positive again.

You can put yourself in a more positive frame of mind about your work by thinking about what you appreciate, just as you can use this process in your personal life to think about what you appreciate generally. After you identify various things you appreciate, pick one that is especially important to you. Focus on that, while experiencing the good feelings flowing into you. (Of course, you can do this with more than one thing you appreciate if you want.)

Use the following chart to help you with this appreciation process. Find a quiet, relaxing place to do this. Even if there are things you don't like about your work or about the people you work with, put them out of your mind, and stay focused on what you *do* appreciate! List as many things as you appreciate, along with your reasons for appreciating them. Try to list at least twelve items. Don't try to analyze or judge your ideas as you do this. Then, go back and rate them on how important they each are to you from 1 (least important) to 3 (most important).

What I Most Appreciate About My Work or Workplace		
What I Appreciate	Why I Appreciate This	Importance (from 1–3)

After you have made your list, go back and review it. Do so in a quiet, relaxed frame of mind. Think of this as a meditation on what you appreciate about your work. Perhaps put on soft, relaxing music in the background and dim the lights, so there is just enough light to see the list. As you look at each item, feel a warm glow of appreciation go through your body.

Then, pick out one of the items on your list that is most important to you and focus on experiencing that. Visualize a screen before you in your mind and see yourself in a scene at work where you are involved in that activity or interacting with that person you really appreciate. And again, let the warm glow of appreciation surge through you, as if you are basking in the sunshine on a beautiful warm day.

You can also use this appreciation technique to appreciate yourself and bolster your feelings of self-esteem and confidence. If there are any qualities you need to develop, you can ask yourself what you want to do, and feel a sense of appreciation that you have this power to make the necessary changes. Use the same process described above for appreciating your work and your workplace. Here's a chart you can use to do this self-appreciation process.

What I Most Appreciate About Myself		
What I Appreciate	Why I Appreciate This	Importance (from 1–3)

Then, after creating your list and rating the importance of each item, review them in a relaxed state of mind, as before. Afterwards, pick the one quality you most appreciate in yourself and visualize yourself in one or more situations where you are exercising that quality.

Finally, if there are qualities you want to develop, use the following chart to list those. Only list up to three qualities, so you can realistically focus on adding those qualities to your repertoire. Then, imagine yourself exercising those qualities, and afterwards decide what you need to do to start working toward putting those qualities into practice in an everyday situation.

Qualities I Want to Develop		
Quality to Develop	Why I Want to Develop This Quality	What I Need to Do to Put This Quality into Practice

Exercising Choice

When you exercise choice you are being proactive and acting from your heart, which gives you a sense of power over your life. When you exercise choice, you feel a sense of autonomy, free will, competence, and self-determination, which increases your feelings of self-esteem and self-confidence.[7] Or as Baker puts it: "Choice is the voice of the heart. It is honesty in action. That's why it's so powerful."[8]

Even when things seem especially difficult and you feel trapped in a situation, such as working in a job that feels oppressive when you are struggling with financial problems, you still have choices. You don't have to be passive and reactive, accepting what comes and trying to make the best of it. Instead, you can be proactive by stopping the process. Reflect on where you are, consider what you want to change, and imagine different scenarios for making changes.

Researchers have found that people can develop a state of psychological stress known as learned helplessness, character- ized by feelings of depression and anxiety, when they feel they don't have any choices.[9] This is a sense of being stuck in a rut from which there is no escape. If you don't feel anxious, you may feel numb, like a zombie, as you try to close off from your feelings of despair. In turn, this state can affect your brain bio- chemistry, triggering even more negative thinking that makes you feel even worse.[10] Moreover, you may start to think the problem is your fault and will last forever, and worse, you may let the problem mushroom into other areas of your life, like seeping pollution. For example, if you find yourself feeling in- competent to do certain tasks at work, you may start to feel you are incompetent to deal with certain issues in your personal life.

Example: George was a sales manager subject to increasing pressures to perform in a declining market. He was expected to make certain quotas, leading him to put more pressure on his salespeople to do more, leading some to quit, making him put even more pressure on himself and on those salespeople who were left. Meanwhile, the declining economy led him to feel he couldn't quit because he wouldn't be able to get another job. He felt increasingly boxed in between his demanding boss and his exasperated employees, who were increasingly resistant to his demands or ready to walk out the door, making him feel even more desperate. He felt harried and haggard. His long hours and anxiety were taking a toll on his marriage, too, since he was often not home and missed some important family occasions.

George did have a number of choices he could make to get out of this box: having an honest talk with his demanding boss to explain the realities of the declining market; reducing his personal expenses to permit him to shift to a less demanding job; recognizing that he didn't need the outward signs of status provided by his current position to be happy; having a heart-to-heart talk with his wife about the situation to see what she might do to help him make changes, and so on.

Sometimes it may feel like you can't do anything when you suddenly feel afraid and panicky, engulfed by negative thoughts, worries, feelings of anger, despair, or the like. But when you suddenly experience such fear reactions, psychologists have found, you actually have a very brief window of time—about ¼ of a second, according to Tara Bennett-Goleman in *Emotional Alchemy*—in which to override the reaction.[11] Then, instead of reacting from fear, as by going along, reacting angrily, or mindlessly fleeing the situation, you can rationally exercise your choice and come up with other options.

There are various ways to deal with this kind of situation to take back your power of choice. When you are in the heat of the situation and you feel ready to act impulsively by lashing out, fleeing, or letting your anger eat you up—at that very moment, you can use a trigger to stop yourself from responding reactively and quickly think of your options to make a choice. Such a trigger can either be a physical signal you create, such as clicking your fingers together as a reminder to stop and choose, or a word or phrase you use through self-talk, which you say to yourself to give yourself this reminder. For example, you could use the phrase "Stop and choose" or something else you want to tell yourself.

Alternatively, take some time away from the situation to reflect on what you want to do to change things. See the situation in your mind and mentally brainstorm different options, write them down, and then go back and review them. Rate them as to what you think would be the most realistic or preferred choices for you. Rate these from 1 to 3, take your top choices, and see them play out on your mental screen. Afterwards, choose which one or combination of options you want to try to make changes. You can use the following chart to help you with the process.

What I Would Like to Change	
Description of Situation:	
Possible Choices	Rating of Choices (from 1–3)

Exercising Your Personal Power

Whatever your position in a company—whether you are in management or an employee—you can still have a sense of exercising your personal power. This is a feeling of being in charge of yourself or what you are doing—not necessarily having power over others. It's a feeling you get when you are doing what you want to be doing, particularly when you feel highly involved or totally absorbed in what you are doing. As Dan Baker, the author of *What Happy People Know*, describes it, this personal power is a "vital force that enables you to be happy with your life, even when it's hard. It comes from the combined power of your intellect and spirit, working in perfect harmony, and it gives you . . . the strength to manage your own emotions, and not let them be dictated by outside forces."[12]

This tool is closely linked to the power of choice and the idea of acceptance, in that your power enables you to choose to either accept what you are experiencing or change your circumstances. Two essential elements of this power are taking responsibility and taking action. You both act and take responsibility for what you think and feel and how you act. In doing so, you put aside any sense of being a victim of what is happening to you. You also don't feel that you have been shortchanged or that you are entitled to a free lunch. You don't feel that you have to wait for someone else to rescue you and you are able to put aside feelings of blaming others. Plus, you feel free to be and act yourself, rather than let someone else dictate how you should act or feel.[13]

In the workplace context, this doesn't mean you don't follow orders; rather that you follow orders because you have chosen to be in this workplace and feel those orders are appropriate and make sense to you. You go along, because it is your choice to do so, because it contributes to harmony in your relationships with others, and so forth. This way, even when you are in the role of a follower, you retain your power.

At the same time, you know you have the power to make another choice when something doesn't feel right to you, such as when you feel an action you are asked to take goes against your personal values or you feel something is unethical or illegal. Then you have a choice to variously stand up for what you believe, leave that workplace, or if you choose to remain, accept that this is the option you have chosen, perhaps because you need the income while you look for another position. But whatever you choose, you are taking an action and the responsibility for that action that goes along with it, so you are acting out of your personal power.

Example: A rookie policeman in Oakland felt uncomfortable when a team of experienced cops working in a high-crime area used their power to browbeat and sometimes beat up suspects, then changed the police reports to cover up or explain away their actions. The situation had been going on for several years, contributing to growing suspicion of the police in much of the community, even while some community members applauded their wild-west frontier version of justice. But in fact many of their actions were illegal and counter to regular police procedures, and after a few weeks of observing this, the rookie cop felt this behavior was wrong—even corrupt—and reported it to higher-ups in the department. The ensuing investigation led to a trial for three of the cops, one of whom fled to Mexico, never to be found again. But while some in the department applauded the rookie's actions as a way to clean out some police officers who went overboard in the pursuit of justice, many others scorned him.

Ultimately he had to leave the department and found a job with the police in another community. From time to time he was called to testify in the ensuing criminal and civil trials that swirled around. The process might have created some difficulties for him with many members of the police department if he had not chosen to leave, but he was acting from his personal power based on his own values of honesty and integrity. By contrast, before he spoke out, he was feeling a sense of stress and disappointment in himself, which commonly occurs when someone doesn't live up to his or her own values. This stress and self-disappointment can lead one to other avenues of escape to wash away the feelings of disappointment and guilt, such as drinking or out-of-control pleasure seeking.

In short, acting from your personal power means being yourself, feeling a sense of commitment to and involvement in whatever you are doing, and acting in accordance with your values. To this end, ask yourself some key questions and write down the answers. Then, if you feel any contradictions between who you are and what you want to do, and between how you appear to others or what you are actually doing, then think about how you might bring those disconnects into better alignment. Likewise, if you feel your values are under siege where you are working or because of the particular tasks you are doing, think about how you might make changes so you feel better and more powerful, whether by choosing acceptance or choosing to make a change.

Some of the questions you might ask are:

- How do I like my job now?

- Is this job contributing to my chosen career path? If not, what can I do about this now?

- What would I really like to do if I could? What can I do now to help to make this happen?

- How do I feel about the people I work with?

- Is there anyone with whom I might better improve my relationship at work? If so, what can I do to improve this?

- What are my core values? What do I value most?

- Are there any conflicts between my most important core values and the values of the people I work with? If so, what are they, and what might I do to change this situation?

As you ask these questions, write down your answers on a sheet of paper, and reflect on what you might do to make any changes and tap into your personal power now.

Tapping into Your Strengths

Building on your talents, abilities, and strengths is another way to increase your happiness, rather than putting your energy into overcoming your problems and weaknesses.[14] Certainly, if a weakness is standing in the way of something you really want to do, you can choose to work on improving in that area if you have a realistic hope of succeeding. But in general, you will get ahead further if you work on developing the areas where you are strongest. There are always stories of how someone overcame a weakness to become great at something, like a frail Teddy Roosevelt became a powerhouse known for his great strength, and became one of the "Rough Riders." Or as another example, told she didn't have the ability to become a good dancer, Merce Cunningham went on to become one of the finest dancers of her generation. But those are the exceptions. Mostly, individuals do best when they capitalize on their strong suits, much like taking advantage of a good hand in poker or bridge to play from strength, rather than hope a bluff will get you through with a weak hand.

Accordingly, if you're choosing a career path or looking for a job, pick something where you can do what you are already good at rather than seeking work in another area where you have to make a major effort to develop new skills. The advantage of doing this is that you gain a competitive edge, much like a company might in choosing to build on its core strengths, rather than diversify into other areas where it is weak. Do what you do well, and not only is success more likely to follow, but you will feel a sense of pleasure and passion in putting your energy into something where success is more assured. Moreover, you will be less fearful, anxious, and tense when you follow your strengths, because you will feel more confident that you know what you are doing and can do it well.

In some cases, you might want to make a career switch to add some variety to your life; but in that case, lower your expectations, so you don't feel you have to perform at the same level as you have doing something where you already have developed strong skills and expertise. You can look on this as an experiment to try something different. Then if you don't find the kind of success you want quickly enough, you can just consider this taking a vacation from what you normally do well, and return to your usual work refreshed.

Example: Let's say that you have had a desk job in administrative work for a long time; you have built a strong skill set around being well organized, good at details, and an excellent researcher in working with data or finding information on the Internet. You may do better looking for a promotion in that area, such as into office management or operations supervisor. If you take a field sales position, your skills would translate well to keeping careful track of sales contact and doing follow-up, but you also have to be outgoing and skilled in working with people. If that isn't one of your strengths, maybe you can't comfortably and quickly develop those skills, in contrast to someone who is a natural salesperson from an early age. So if you do try it out, don't be disappointed if you can't perform as well as you hoped. Rather than take the plunge into what are likely to be chilly waters, you may be better off to stay in the warmer waters and hone your skills there. This will help you get further ahead, as well as building your feelings of self-esteem and personal power, because you are doing what you know you do well. It simply feels good when you are able to perform well.

This kind of conflict between acting from your strength versus overcoming your weaknesses is particularly likely to arise when you have someone else encouraging you to do something that plays to your weaknesses rather than your strengths. For instance, you are perfectly comfortable working as a techie, because you like working with equipment and data, but a parent or spouse is pressuring you to go into sales or management because it pays better or has a more powerful image. That's when you should draw on your personal power and ability to choose to say "no," so you stay with your strengths. Don't let someone else's vision draw you into working from a position of weakness.

By the same token, if you've experienced some difficult problems, losses, or traumas in your life, don't dwell on them to try to resolve them. In some schools of psychology, the approach is to work on talking about or working through past problems with the idea of confronting them in order to overcome them. But positive psychologists have found that such a focus only keeps you stuck in the past, like rehashing old wounds and picking at unhealed sores. You just end up feeling worse and can easily see yourself as a victim, which is anathema to feeling joyous and happy. Instead, look to the future and focus on what's working in your life so you feel better. As Dan Baker explains it: "When you focus on problems . . . you become bogged down in your own negativity and fear. It's much smarter to focus on possibilities."[15] That way you can literally leapfrog over your problems.

A parallel with this process of working from your individual strength is the notion of finding the "best practices" for a company, sometimes called the company's "core competencies." These are the activities where a company can perform most efficiently and generate the most profit. Finding what companies do best, assessing where they achieve the highest level of excellence, is what Tom Peters wrote about in selecting companies to profile in his classic, *In Search of Excellence.* As companies have found again and again, they are most likely to thrive in a competitive marketplace when they do what they do most effectively. When they try to diversify too much, they can dilute their ability to perform well. This is what occurred when Time-Warner tried to expand into the Internet by acquiring AOL. The idea was to expand its media empire onto another platform, but instead, the merger only dragged the company down during a high-tech meltdown when stock prices that were built on illusionary dreams of future growth didn't materialize.

So what are your own strengths? What are the areas where you shine? And which of these areas do you prefer working in or want to further develop? After you answer these questions, review your strengths and reflect on how you have used these strengths in the past and how you might further put them into practice in the future. This way, you can both enjoy thinking about what you do well and think of ways to better build on your strengths in the future. You can use the chart below to help you do this.

What Are My Biggest Strengths? What Do I Do Best?		
My Strengths	How Am I Using My Strengths Now at Work	Strength of My Strengths (from 1–5)

After you have listed your strengths and how you have used them, go back and rate them as to their importance for you from

1–5. Or if you prefer, rate them according to the strength of each of these strengths from 1–5. This way you can select your abilities or talents that are the most powerful for you.

Then, take your most powerful or important strengths and reflect on them one at a time, asking the question: "How can I use this strength to enhance my work or career in the future?" Don't try to answer the question intellectually. Rather, let the answers come to you, as you relax and visualize how you might use this strength to your advantage in the future.

Using Language and Stories to Be Happier

The words you use and the stories you tell can also affect your happiness. According to the Sapir-Whorf hypothesis for natural language, commonly taught in introductory psychology for decades, the language we use helps determine how we view and think about the world. It both restricts what we see and expands our vision. The classic example is the Eskimos having dozens of words for snow, so they are attuned to the many ways that snow appears and what this means for living their life.

By the same token, the words you use in talking to others and in self-talk shape your own view of the world and how people respond to you. So if you use "happy talk," essentially framing what you say in a positive perspective, that's how you'll perceive the world and how others will perceive who you are.

For example, if you are given a task and tell yourself "I can't do this" or "I shouldn't be doing this," your thoughts will hold you back from performing the task. If you think, "It may be hard, but I can do this," you may very well find you can do it. Likewise, if you have thoughts like, "This is boring" or "People just don't get me," you'll find that your feelings and perceptions come to pass as well. Your negative thoughts trigger your own feelings of unhappiness.

By contrast, when you use positive language to guide your

thinking, such as telling yourself that "this could be interesting" or "I'm a unique person with a rare combination of skills," your words help to prepare the way for you to feel happy. They set the stage for you to have positive experiences, even when you are engaged in routine activities, or for you to feel assured and confident that things will turn out well, even when you are doing something new and challenging or meeting people for the first time. That's what psychologist Dan Baker has found in helping to change the perspective of clients from negative to positive. As he notes:

> "People who are stuck in fear are often fixated on destructive language. Their conversations are full of "can't," "don't," "shouldn't," and "won't." They also tend to describe their own actions in the passive voice, instead of the active. In addition, they ask questions that beg for negative responses . . .
>
> However, I've noticed that when people begin to change, their language changes, too. The negatives fall away, the passive descriptions are replaced by active ones, and the "no" questions give way to "yes" questions."[16]

Likewise, you can change the language you use and, by doing so, change the way you perceive and think about things. For example, if you view a difficult situation or problem as a possibility or opportunity, it changes the way you will approach that situation or problem. You will look for solutions or benefits to be achieved, rather than feeling stuck and complaining about what happened. At the same time, you want to avoid unrealistic affirmations, like telling yourself again and again that "I am a million-dollar winner." You want your self-talk, your positive thoughts about what you can do and achieve, to be realistic and achievable. You need to use them as guidelines for actually moving toward your goal. While positive thoughts can help ease your way to achievement, you still have to *act* to get where you want to go.

Similarly, the stories you tell yourself or others shape your experiences and the way others perceive you. For example, when you tell yourself or others about positive experiences, without exaggerating or distorting the truth, you contribute to having a happy outlook on life. If your descriptions are full of complaints and express your fears and feelings of paranoia and helplessness, they will help to pull you down. Moreover, as much as people may enjoy hearing a dramatic tale of conflict and tragedy from time to time, they still like hearing the uplifting, soar-to-success ending. So if you are continually the bearer of bad news and complaints, people will pull away.

Example: I had that experience myself when I first met a wannabe producer from Los Angeles. Though she was involved in a spiritual practice that helped her relax and feel more optimistic and better about herself, her stories were filled with problems and paranoia. She repeatedly told me and others stories of her difficult childhood, complained about her ineffective mother and abandoning father, and she repeatedly described the difficulties of getting to see powerful movers and shakers in a hard, unforgiving town. And she often described experiences of people stealing this or that project, leading her to speak in generalities about how people lie, cheat, and can't be trusted.

Since I was eager to make some connections in the town, I found her introductions helpful, but gradually I began to see how her negative vision led her to act self-destructively again and again. She shot herself in the foot repeatedly, just as she was on the verge of accomplishing something. Her feelings of distrust led her into conflicts with people who were trying to help her, so she pushed away the very people she needed to make a project happen, and so again and again her dreams died. Yet, she was too myopic to see it was her own self-destructive actions, fueled by her own perceptions and stories, which led to these calamities again and again.

By contrast, a woman I met at a screenplay-writers workshop, who spoke about how to network your way to success in Hollywood, had a cheery, outgoing personality that drew people to her. She combined that with a talent for writing, to make the personal connections she needed to sell dozens of scripts and get hired as a writer or consultant on dozens of projects.

Whatever your experiences, look at ways to recast them in a positive, optimistic light. For example, if you find a boss or a client is critical of some work you have done, don't tell yourself that you are close to losing your job or your client. Instead, tell yourself that you are fortunate to have a boss or client who is willing to give you feedback to help you improve—and think about ways you can take that feedback to heart to do a bang-up job in the future. Then, instead of acting defensively at the criticism, trying to show that what you did wasn't so bad after all or attacking them for not understanding your vision, show your appreciation for their feedback and point out how you will incorporate it in reworking what you did. Generally, this kind of approach will win you fans and a more positive reception when you again present your material, even when the actual changes you make are few. While such optimism may not work every time, in the long run, using positive language and positive stories will pay off with more positive results—and you'll feel much happier along the way.

Creating a Fuller Life

Still another way to be happier is to live a full, multidimensional life; look for happiness not only in work, but in other areas of your life as well. Then, your happiness in other areas will enhance your happiness in work. Even if you are still struggling with finding as much happiness as you want at work, your happiness in other areas will contribute to your feeling more positive about whatever difficulties you are having at work. Remember the "don't put all your eggs in one basket approach," which investors are advised to use in diversifying their opportunities. Well, the same approach works in bringing happiness into your life. Keep things more diversified and interesting by seeking happiness in several complementary areas; you will find that the sum is likely to be greater than its parts, as the combination results in an exponential growth in happiness for you.

I recall jumping rope back in elementary school to the saying: "All work and no play makes Jack a dull boy." That's absolutely true. Single-minded focus on anything—even on something exciting—makes you dull not only to others but also to yourself, since it can contribute to feelings of stress and tension. As psychologist Dan Baker describes it: "Millions of people kill themselves by putting all their energy into just one dimension of life—usually work—and end up with the disease I call unidimensional living: a one-track life. It's fatal—not always physically, but it's fatal."[17]

So find ways to diversify whatever you are doing, because as much as you may feel you like doing it, too much of a good thing can turn into a rut; and the more you do it, the deeper the rut. So whether it's a hobby, a pet, a relationship, an extended vacation, whatever, find other things that are fulfilling for you to expand the dimensions of your life beyond your work. You can use the following chart to help you determine what these are—and whether you need to pay more attention to them or add them to your life.

Avoiding the Happiness Traps

Finally, as you work toward being happier, you want to avoid the happiness traps that may seem seductive—like the sirens in *The Odyssey* who sought to lure Odysseus and his men off their path home—but in the long run are illusory and destructive of becoming truly happy. These are:

What Other Dimensions Besides Work Are Important to Me and Can I Add Them to My Life?			
Other Activities or Relationships	What Part or Percent of My Life Are These Now?	Importance to Me (from 1–3)	How Can I Increase or Add This in My Life?

1. *The Lure of Money, Where You Think You Can Buy Happiness with Wealth.* Certainly, you need a basic amount of money so you feel secure and can live comfortably. But beyond that, seeking money for its own sake or for status can lead you into the trap of wanting more and more or piling up more possessions than you can reasonably use. It may feel natural to seek more and more—in the financial field, for example, accumulating money, stocks, and other instruments of wealth are like a scoreboard of how you are doing. But the process can turn you into a slave of

your money and possessions, so you feel worried about losing them and protecting them.

One big danger of pursuing money for its own sake is finding yourself trapped in a job you don't like, even though it pays very well. You are essentially trapped by your own success and you can find yourself feeling empty despite all your possessions. And even your leisure time can turn into a kind of empty escapism, like a prisoner on a weekend pass, because you feel otherwise stuck. Wealthy celebrities who seem to have everything, but then end up with serious problems of drug addiction, alcoholism, and who even commit or attempt suicide, are clear examples of how money, fame, status, and power don't buy happiness. People who seem to have everything may feel they have nothing, because they don't have the happiness that comes from the happiness qualities, like having a sense of purpose, having good relationships, and so on.

2. *The Pursuit of Pleasure.* While seeking pleasure from time to time can be great, it can become a trap if you pursue it too much, just like a drug can give a high but can turn into a destructive addiction. You can, as psychologists describe it, end up on the "hedonic treadmill,"[18] where you keep seeking out pleasure like an addict. The problem is that after a while, too much pleasure can become dull and boring; it loses its novelty and ability to stimulate and excite. It becomes like the vacation that goes on too long, so it ceases to be a vacation; the sweet dessert that loses its good taste if you eat too much. Pursue pleasure in moderation, so it is like an occasional celebration or festival that adds zest to your life. But don't try to turn what should be a punctuation mark into the whole sentence—or you'll turn the pursuit of pleasure into a trap.

The other traps only need to be touched on briefly, since they have already been mentioned.

3. *Trying to Find Happiness by Resolving the Past.* The effort to be happy by working through what has happened to you in the

past is often a dead end. Rather, as previously discussed, it is best to let the past go, whereby you remember but forgive others, learn from bad experiences, and move on. If you dwell on the past you will be stuck there.

4. *Overcoming Your Weaknesses, Rather Than Developing Your Strengths.* Another trap is working on overcoming your weaknesses as a way to be happy. Whenever you focus on the negative, you just give that more attention and energy; instead you should focus on your strengths, which is where you are more likely to achieve. As researchers going back to B. F. Skinner have found, rewards work better than punishments in conditioning and reinforcing a desired behavior.[19] That's why you'll find dozens of books on ways to reward employees at work, to motivate them and create incentives for better performance and increased productivity. But you won't find any books on different ways to punish employees to get them to do a better job.

5. *Forcing Yourself to Be Happy.* Finally, you can't simply make yourself be happy by deciding that you will be happy. Rather, you need to seek to achieve the key qualities of happiness previously noted (such as love, optimism, being proactive, and having a sense of purpose) and use the tools (such as appreciation, choice, and expressing your personal power) that will help you achieve that happiness.

3

What Makes People Happy?

After dozens of years of research and hundreds of research studies, psychologists and others studying what brings satisfaction and happiness have come up with findings about what makes people happy. Here in brief are some of the major findings, many of them noted in *100 Simple Secrets of Happy People: What Scientists Have Learned and How You Can Use It* by David Niven, who has reviewed over 1,000 studies describing the characteristics and attitudes of happy people.[1]

While many of these principles may seem obvious, the kind of things I recall being told as I was growing up by my parents and teachers, it is also helpful to know that these observations have been supported by scientific research through surveys and psychological experiments. The studies have titles like "The Relationship between Job Satisfaction and Life Satisfaction,"[2] "Testing for Stress and Happiness: The Role of Social and Cognitive Factors,"[3] and "Optimism and Pessimism and Partially Independent Constructs: Relationship to Positive and Negative Affectivity and Psychological Well-Being."[4] In general, the findings have been confined to academics and professionals in the emerging field of positive psychology. But once translated into everyday English, they provide suggestions on what we can do to increase our happiness in work and everyday life.

Your Overall Attitude Toward Work and Life

- You will be happier if you feel your life is purposeful and meaningful. If you don't have a sense of purpose, the activities you do may seem meaningless and you may feel empty and adrift.

- You will also be happier if you feel a sense of connection to others.

- Look toward things other than money to make you happy. Once you have enough money for security and comfort, those other qualities are the most important sources of satisfaction. (See Chapter 1 for a detailed listing of what these other qualities are.)

- Seek to do things that make you happy, so you allow and encourage yourself to feel happy; people who are unhappy continue to do things that make them unhappy.

- Your goals should complement or be aligned with each other, so you feel a sense of harmony as you work toward your goals. By contrast, if your goals are contradictory, this can create personal conflicts that detract from your happiness.

- Choose goals that fit with your view of who you are, and don't try to set goals that really aren't important to you or are goals that someone else has proposed for you. You can choose what game you want to play and win; if you don't want to play, don't try to win.

- Choose the goals you want to choose, not the goals that others choose for you. You'll be happier when you are working

WHAT MAKES PEOPLE HAPPY? ◎ 39

toward goals you really want to achieve for yourself, not for someone else.

• As long as your goals are meaningful, reasonable, and aligned, work enthusiastically toward achieving them; you'll feel happy as you move toward them.

• Keep your expectations realistic, so you aren't disappointed. Happiness doesn't come from getting everything you want, but from wanting most of what you get. So if your goals are modest and realistic, you are likely to achieve them; if your goals are too high, you are setting yourself up for failure and disappointment.

• Be open and flexible, so you are continually learning and adapting to new ideas, since the world is constantly changing. Don't feel you have to achieve goals you have already set if conditions have changed.

• Be ready to revise your goals and set new ones to adapt to changes in your personal situation, expectations, values, and assessment of what's most important to you. Just like marketers have to continually change and adapt their products to respond to changes in society, so you need to be ready to change as well; otherwise, you will feel increasingly upset and frustrated, as change occurs and leaves you behind.

• When you do make changes, allow yourself some time to make the adjustment to your new circumstances. Just as you should be flexible with the situation in making changes, you should be flexible with yourself, so you can more comfortably and happily adapt to change.

• Diversify your sources of satisfaction and pleasure, so if you have problems in one area—whether in your work or your personal life—you can still find joy and satisfaction in other areas.

- Don't seek perfection in one area of your life at the expense of other areas. You'll be happier if everything is generally going well than if you've lavished your efforts on making one part of your life perfect, while the rest of your life is a mess.

- In fact, don't seek to be perfect. Complete perfection is impossible, since it's always possible to make something better. Instead, try to improve and be the best that you can, so you appreciate what you do and can achieve, rather than feeling disappointed at what is unattainable and ever out of reach.

- Be yourself, based on what you feel comfortable doing and being, rather than feeling you have to be like everyone else. Choose the work you want to do accordingly, to best suit your unique attributes and personality.

- Lower your threshold for defining whether your experiences are positive or negative ones. The more likely you are to characterize an experience of any type as positive rather than negative, the more likely you are to have more positive experiences, so you feel happier and more satisfied with your life and your work.

- Look on any setbacks or disappointments as temporary events; that way you realize that any feelings of upset will pass, because of the healing power of time. So rather than dwelling on any negative situation that has occurred, shift your attention to other things or to the future.

- If you are more of a big-picture type of person, think of your overall accomplishments in life or at work. You'll especially enjoy thinking about your life and work achievements in general. If you tend to home in on the details, think more about the specific achievements that have been especially important to you; you'll enjoy savoring each detail.

- Believe that in the long run, goodness and justice will win out, so you retain an optimistic frame of mind. Thus, even if you experience some injustice or unfairness, recognize that the person who did this will ultimately pay the consequences in some form—whether by your actions, by the actions of someone else, or by something they do to themselves. Consider this karma—the law of cause and effect—and if you remind yourself that this law really works, you will feel happier.

Your Attitude Toward Yourself

- Accept yourself for who you are; don't judge yourself negatively by the amount of money you make, where you live, or the work you do. Appreciate yourself for being the unique you, whatever your particular abilities and talents and limitations.

- Believe in yourself and in your own abilities to accomplish what you realistically seek to do; your "I can" beliefs will help you do what you set out to do. At the same time, don't expect yourself to be perfect, because everyone makes mistakes. You should be open to learn from others and accept constructive criticism. That way you not only have confidence in what you can do now, but confidence that you can always adapt and learn to do it better.

- Just as you embrace yourself, embrace your own ethnic or racial heritage, which is part of what makes you you. This connection can also give you a sense of your own history and place in the world.[5]

- Learn to appreciate where you are now and what you have accomplished, rather than feeling disappointed that you haven't done more. You can always look to the future to seek further accomplishments; just be appreciative for who you are now and honor your talents and abilities.

- By the same token, learn to appreciate what you have, rather than being concerned about what you don't have or can't have or what others have; you'll feel happier that way.

- Don't get stuck thinking about what could or might have been if you had done something differently. Getting caught up in regrets will only make you feel bad, because you are unable to make changes in what happened in the past. Instead, focus on what you might learn from that experience or how you might change in the future, because you can make positive changes there.

- Put your attention on things that are positive for you as much as possible. Though you can't always avoid thinking about a negative experience or person, try to keep such thoughts to a minimum, because you will feel happier. By contrast, people who dwell on things that are negative are likely to feel less satisfied and content.

- Avoid blaming yourself if things go wrong. Getting caught up in self-blame is not only unproductive in resolving the problem but can make it more difficult for you to function effectively. Typically, difficult situations arise because of a number of factors, including some things you can't control. So focus on resolving the problem in the here and now, rather than trying to assess blame for what has occurred in the past.

Your Attitude Toward Your Work

- When you think of your work, appreciate what you gain from it, and think less about what is wrong with it. For example, think of how work gives you a sense of purpose, helps you develop certain skills, and contributes to your feelings of self-esteem and confidence, rather than complaining about how you feel you aren't paid enough for what you do.

• Remind yourself that you always have choices, so you are always free to make decisions and choose. So if you don't like what you are doing, you can change it, do something different, leave, or change your attitude. You might feel better about what you are doing if you consider that it is helping to give you the money you need, is a step on a career path, or because you can feel detached and project your mind someplace else while you work.

• Act in accordance with your values and morals in seeking to achieve your goals. If you compromise what you believe in, you will have feelings of disappointment and dissatisfaction.

• If you are feeling down about something, keep believing in yourself and don't give up. Just see any rejection as a challenge, so work on doing whatever it is better next time.

• Seek to better understand yourself by being aware of your feelings and what you like and don't like doing. Then, if you feel down about something, you can more accurately assess why you are feeling that way, so you can better know what to do to perk up your mood.

Your Relationships to Others

• You'll be happier if you aren't supercompetitive, so you don't feel you have to "win" all the time. The fact is that highly competitive people who feel compelled to excel or even win at whatever they do tend to enjoy things less.

- Be outwardly cheery when you are around others, and not only will your positive outlook rub off on others, who will reflect your enthusiasm back, but it will help you feel better, too. In fact, it's a great pick-me-up if you are feeling down yourself.

- Smile often, because your smile will not only make you feel happier, but others will tend to mimic your expression, which will boost their spirits as well, contributing to increased harmony and happiness in the workplace as a whole.

- Be agreeable and easy to get along with. Think about what you like about the people you work with rather than being difficult to deal with and critical of others, even if you have the power to express your anger or enforce your demands on others. In the long run, you'll find people more cooperative and eager to please you when you use sweetness and honey, rather than vinegar and a two-by-four.

- Don't compare yourself to people who have more money or have achieved more. Don't let other people's accomplishments get you down, whether these are co-workers, friends, family members, or acquaintances you barely know at all. While it can be fine to use people with more success as a role model in setting your goals to achieve, you don't want to use the comparison to make yourself feel bad about what you haven't yet achieved. Ideally, in making comparisons with others, choose examples that are "meaningful but that make you feel comfortable with who you are and what you have."[6]

- Develop friendships at work or with neighbors to help you feel connected to others and to help you feel part of a larger whole. Being a part of a social organization is a key aspect of being human; you are happier when you have this sense of connection, where you care about others and feel they care about you.

- Seek out good relationships with others, from family and friends to co-workers and neighbors. As researchers have found, relationships, rather than having a lot of money, are more important to happiness.[7]

- Give others and everyday situations the benefit of the doubt, when you are uncertain. Think of positive possibilities rather than looking for hidden agendas and evil intentions or thinking that things will go wrong. In general, seek to trust others—if you expect things to go right, they usually will. Your positive, trusting attitude will help you be happier.

- Show others you care about them and appreciate them, and you are likely to evoke similar responses from them in return. The result is you will have stronger relationships, because relationships "build on mutual appreciation."[8] Since good relationships are at the core of what makes us happy, this will add to your happiness quotient, too.

- Should you run into difficulties, don't feel you have to resolve them alone. Look to others for support in finding solutions. Not only will their input and assistance help you feel better, but you will have an outside perspective that may contribute to resolving the problem.

- Similarly, share your feelings, ideas, hopes, and dreams with others, so you feel more connected to them. You'll also feel happier, even if you encounter difficulties or challenges or things don't go your way, because you have more support from others.

- Find ways to contribute to or help others, such as volunteering in your community. As you give to others, you will feel happier, and you will feel better about yourself. You will feel more purposeful and will gain appreciation from others for your generous acts. In addition, volunteering can be a way to learn and do new things, making your life more interesting and vital.

- If others you are close to need help or support, be willing to help out. You will both further your relationship and make yourself feel better, since being altruistic and helpful to others feels good.

- Treat others respectfully and avoid becoming overly aggressive in making your point, even when you are right. You will be happier if you seek to get along with others at the same time that you seek to get your way; less happy when you aggressively achieve a win while alienating others in your wake. While you may win a particular battle, in the long run, you may lose the war, as well as undermine your feelings of happiness, too.

- Should problems arise between people you are working with—or in your personal life—seek to help the people work in harmony again. Help them cool down their emotions and work on overcoming the problem in a reasonable way.

- When you have critical words to say to someone or seek some behavioral change on their part, frame what you say in a positive, constructive way. Rather than focusing on what the person has done wrong, point out what the person can do that's right or better. In turn, you'll find others more receptive to receiving your criticism, less likely to get defensive, and more likely to change in a way that you want.

Working Smarter and Better

- To increase your efficiency at work and to feel more in control and confident, develop a realistic schedule or routine to use in doing your work. That'll help you know what you are doing and divide up larger projects into a series of doable tasks. However, you should still be flexible and open to change as needed. View your schedule as a guideline, but not a rigid guide as to what to do.

- Intend to keep the promises you make, so if you make a promise and say you are going to do something, follow through. That way people will trust you, and you will also feel secure and confident in yourself. Otherwise, you will find that empty promises can lead to failed projects and people will lose their enthusiasm for working with you, because they doubt your word and commitment to do what you say.

- Commit yourself to completing whatever you start and to doing well whatever you do. You'll feel good at doing a good job, even if you are the only one who knows how good it is. While it can sometimes be tempting to drop the ball and do something else, you may be left with feelings of disappointment and feel incomplete about not fulfilling your commitment to do something and do it well.

- Having a lot to do tends to go with being happy, as long as you don't feel overwhelmed by having *too* much to do. It's better to have a full schedule with plenty to do than to have extra time on your hands and feel unchallenged or bored.

- Where possible, look on your job as a calling or at least a step on the career ladder rather than just a job. This way, you make your job a way of expressing who you are, so you feel more satisfied and fulfilled whatever you are doing.

- Seek to do something every day where you can feel a sense of accomplishment or improvement, even if the amount of accomplishment or improvement is relatively small. It will help you feel you are progressing toward a particular goal and give you a sense of satisfaction for the progress you have been able to make.

- Where possible, do what you do well; you're more likely to excel when you play to your strengths and feel competent at the tasks you are performing.

- If you find a problem or conflict unimportant or seemingly impossible to resolve, let it go. Otherwise, you'll find it frustrating and enervating trying to deal with that problem or conflict; it's better to spend your time on something where you can achieve a successful result.

- Keep a small notebook and pen readily available so you can jot down ideas you have. Not only will you be able to capture good ideas you might otherwise forget, but you'll feel more on top of things. By writing things down, you will often have at your fingertips something you can easily use as needed. And others will appreciate your being a repository for these sudden bits of knowledge.

Miscellaneous Tips on Being Happy

- Don't measure your success by your material possessions. Once you are able to live comfortably, don't be unduly swayed by status symbols, like having an expensive car or big house. Consider them add-ons, and remember what really contributes to happiness are your personal resources, such as your friends, family, and co-workers.[9]

- Stay fit and healthy by eating well, exercising, and getting a good night's sleep. If your body is in better condition, you will feel better, have more energy for your work, and enjoy whatever you are doing more.

- Find ways to bring humor and laughter into the workplace. Breaking up the routine increases performance, productivity, and creativity, because people enjoy their work more. If your company doesn't already have special events like contests, dress-up days, and the like, see if you can add them to the mix.

- Aside from having fun in the workplace, find some other time during the day to do something you consider really fun.

- Take some time to remember the happy times you have had in the past—at work or in your personal life. You'll not only enjoy reminiscing, but your recollections will contribute to a continued happy mood in the present.

- Find ways to have fun doing whatever might normally be routine, such as by turning a chore or repetitive job into a game, thinking about something pleasant while you do a routine task, or enjoying an interaction with someone while you are doing the job.

PART II

Break Down the Barriers to Enjoyment

4

Assess Where You Are Now

What can you do to enjoy life more? What stands in the way? By increasing your enjoyment of life generally, you will have more energy and enthusiasm to bring to your work. And your overall upbeat positive attitude will contribute to having a better outlook and attitude at work.

Getting Started Now

Since a good starting point is assessing where you are now, I begin by asking a number of people three questions: "What keeps you from enjoying things?" "What can you do to enjoy life more?" and "What do you enjoy doing the most now?" Here are some representative responses.

A Woman Working in a Series of Mid-Level Jobs

Andrea is thirty-eight and has been working in a series of mid-level administrative, clerical, and service jobs. Her responses were typical. Most recently, she had worked as a counselor for troubled teens, a loan advisor for new homeowners, and a data entry clerk, while starting a small sales business at trade shows. But nothing fully satisfied her, and she was still looking for a job to which she could fully commit. Meanwhile, in her personal life, she had a very close relationship with her mother, who she saw almost every day, and a stormy relationship with a sister who lived with her mother between boyfriends. Regardless of what Andrea felt inside, outwardly she had a chipper, bubbly personality, which covered up her feelings of dissatisfaction and concern.

In response to my first question, "What keeps you from enjoying things?", Andrea mentioned her job and financial limitations, which might lead to other questions, such as why did she take this job and how could she overcome these financial limitations or find alternative means of enjoyment. When I asked: "What can you do to enjoy life more?" many of her answers could easily apply to many other people:

- Be more positive.

- Help others.

- Spend more time with others.

- Work in the community.

- Contribute to the happiness of others.

- Don't worry so much about what others think.

- Believe in yourself.

I noticed that many of Andrea's responses focused around being with and helping others, a focus further confirmed when I asked her: "What is your dream? What do you really want to do?" Her answers centered around making others happy, such as her comment: "I'd like to see people get along and see the world a happier place, with a lack of hatred and racism." Yet, since Andrea also felt a lack of internal peace and satisfaction, I suggested playing The Mirror Game, in which she should imagine herself standing in front of a mirror and play a brainstorming game. "Just ask yourself the question: 'What makes me happy? What do I most enjoy doing now?'"

Then, with this mirror image in mind, Andrea began brainstorming—"Doing things for others" . . . "Don't think about it . . . Just go do it." . . . "Try not to have any regrets; just do things and don't look back." Then, as she reflected on her comments, Andrea explained how her mostly positive attitude helped her deal with and enjoy many things, even when things were going wrong, by thinking that everything would work out in the end.

Yet, sometimes this largely positive, optimistic attitude and helpful, giving spirit wasn't enough. I suggested some ways she could further increase her enjoyment. For example, she could try to find a more fulfilling job and she could feel more satisfaction in some things she was already doing, such as going to church. This was the beginning of a journey to help Andrea find ways to get rid of the difficulties she faced and think about what changes to make in light of her real limitations.

A Hard-Driving Sales Executive

Another person needing an enjoyment makeover was forty-six-year-old Barry, a hard-driving sales executive for a manufacturer. Outwardly, he was the epitome of success, with a top-paying job, a beautiful suburban home, an attractive, loyal wife, and three kids, from eight to thirteen, all doing well in school. Yet, inside, Barry was a Type-A personality who couldn't relax and simply enjoy things. Instead, he spent much of life creating tasks and deadlines for himself and others, pushing himself from one activity to another, and worrying if his effort was enough. Would he meet his sales quotas? Would his company throttle the competition? He was like a general seeking to win a war each day, and when he went home, he took that high tension with him. He found it hard to relax and enjoy anything, since even during leisure activities, he was still thinking about what he would do tomorrow and the next day, week, and month. Even at social events with his wife, he would wear his sales hat, thinking about whether any people there could provide yet another lead for his sales force.

Thus, for Barry, his leisure-time activities brought him no pleasure. He acted like he was enjoying himself, but he really wasn't. So while he might answer the question: "What do you enjoy most?" with a list of recreational activities, he doesn't really enjoy them. His answer of "working fewer hours" to the question, "What can you do to enjoy life more?" is just the beginning of the search. Barry has to do more than redirect hours from the work to the leisure category. He needs an attitude makeover to fully enjoy his leisure activities, and he needs to find new leisure-time activities as well, activities that he truly enjoys for themselves, not just as another venue for prospecting clients.

A Couple Overwhelmed by Owning a Small Business

In another case, Susan and Jacob, a couple in their forties, took over a bar and nightclub, despite having no experience, because they loved the local rock scene. Before, both had been high-school teachers and had enjoyed coming to the club to listen to music, but the crowds had grown sparser, leaving the club on the brink of bankruptcy. Thinking the club would be fun to manage, they took it over with the help of a silent partner who owned a small manufacturing business. After they changed the type of music played, the club took off, and the crowd grew into the hundreds on Friday and Saturday nights.

But while Susan and Jacob were thrilled their club was doing so well, what had once been an enjoyable, exciting new venture became exhausting, overwhelming, and no longer fun. So for them, a clear solution was finding a buyer or otherwise getting out of the club. Even if they had to take a financial loss, they had to literally stop the music—since it was now stopping them from enjoying what they were doing.

Discovering a New Attitude Toward Enjoyment

These stories of Andrea, Barry, Susan and Jacob, and many other people I interviewed illustrate that fully enjoying what you are doing—from work to leisure activities—is not just about *what* you are doing, but is about your *attitude* toward these activities and how you are able to balance your work and personal life. Two people can participate in the same activity, and while one might find it intensely fulfilling, the other might find it dull and routine. Also, what is deeply satisfying at one time may become a tedious, boring, time-consuming activity, if one's interest has shifted to other things.

Since the source of joy and fun in an activity can come from many different places, being aware of these sources can help you tap into them, like finding a secret spring of enjoyment, as well as prioritizing and balancing what you want to do. I noticed this when I went to a friend's party and asked people to describe what they especially enjoyed and why. As they shared thoughts about what they did, I noticed that it wasn't the activity itself but the enthusiasm or positive attitude they brought to it that was the key.

For example, when Cindy, a transportation supervisor in her thirties, described how much she liked going to a toy store to buy things for herself, she emphasized that what she most enjoyed was the feeling of being a child again. She said, "I love going to a toy store for myself, since it makes me feel like a kid again, like when I went to the store and bought some dolls for myself. I bought an Elmo doll and a Winnie the Pooh doll. Just looking at them brings a smile to my face, whenever I feel sad about something. I just look at them and grin all over. It's like when I was a child and had no cares."

Eliciting positive feedback from others was another source of enjoyment. For example, Judy, a receptionist in her forties, perked up her daily walks when she smiled at a stranger and got a smile or friendly remark in return. As she described it: "Sometimes I really enjoy it when I smile at a stranger. Even if the person might think I'm crazy, it makes me feel good all over, just to smile like that, and when a stranger smiles back, I feel even better."

In the same spirit, Judy said that she liked helping others because of their positive, appreciative responses. She also felt empowered by her own strength, since she had something to give, noting that: "I find it very enjoyable to volunteer and give food to poor kids. It makes me feel good helping them, and I feel so blessed that I have what I have, when these kids have no place to call their home."

Likewise, seventy-year-old Jerry found a great satisfaction contributing to others as a volunteer at a local hospital. Though his tasks there were routine office paperwork, his joy came from feeling he was contributing and being part of a high-spirited group that liked doing things together, such as planning a holiday party for the volunteers, patients, doctors, and nurses.

Others I spoke to described how a particular event or activity tapped some positive emotional chord, such as being exciting, relaxing, amusing, challenging, or intriguing.

So, when you assess how to add more enjoyment to your life, don't just look at what activities you enjoy doing, but consider your reasons for finding those activities enjoyable. Then, you can seek ways to apply those factors in the future. The many techniques and games in this book will show you how.

Doing Your Own Enjoyment Assessment

To start thinking about how to add this enjoyment, assess where you are now and track how you are doing over the next few days or weeks. This assessment will help you focus your attention on what you find more or less enjoyable, so you can work on reducing what's less enjoyable and increasing what's more enjoyable in your work and your life. To this end, keep an *"ENJOY!* Journal," in which you focus on what you find enjoyable and what you don't. Then, use that information to reduce or eliminate what you are doing that you don't enjoy—or don't enjoy as much—while increasing what you do enjoy. You may want to make a game out of keeping this journal by awarding yourself gold stars or adding asterisks for what you like doing, and give yourself black circles or a minus sign for what you don't like to do.

When you start your *ENJOY!* Journal, write about what you enjoy or don't enjoy in general, and note what you do to make an activity more enjoyable. Then, rate the different activities you do, using the ENJOY-O-METER scale that goes from 0 (not very enjoyable at all) to 10 (really great!). Additionally, provide an overall rating for all these activities each day. In doing so, put down the first thought that comes to mind, since that will better reflect your initial intuitive or gut reaction. Take ten to twenty minutes at the end of the day to do this. While it's ideal to keep the journal every day, you can do a summary for the past two or three days if a daily record becomes a problem.

Review your journal every week or two to reflect back on your experiences, using some of the techniques and games you'll learn in subsequent chapters. This reflection will help you analyze how much you enjoy the different activities you are engaged in, so you can decide what to do more or less of, thereby charting more fun times into your life.

You can use a regular journal book and make your entries by hand or make the entries in a journal you create on your computer. Here are a few of my own journal entries to show how you might code different activities.

ENJOY! Journal (12-19-04)

Today, I was really enthusiastic about writing a kid's book (10) and I truly enjoyed the holiday party at Bill's (9), where I really enjoyed talking and listening to people . . . All in all, a great event.

I was supposed to critique a really bad novel, which I didn't feel like doing (3). But I spaced it out before and after watching the great new show *Desperate Housewives* (10). Then, I updated the "Kids' Mistakes" Web site (8) and wrote and sent out a press release about the project (8).

Overall, about a 9 day.

ENJOY! Journal (12-21-04)

Today, I'm catching up for Monday and Tuesday. On Monday, I finishing up reading and writing a synopsis for the awful book (3), but got it done. Then, I polished up my resume and applied for a teaching job (5), worked on publisher and agent updates (4), and went to a dinner at a Cambodian restaurant with some members of a social club. There was a lot of interest in my kids project and work in school, so felt very charged up by the occasion (9)

Then, Tuesday, after sending out some queries for clients (4), making phone calls to follow-up on interest in some of my scripts (5), I spent some time watching TV—*Billionaire* and *High School Reunion* (8), and made space to dance and exercise again (9).

Overall, about a 7 for today.

Starting Your Own *ENJOY!* Journal

The above is just a sampling of the journal I started keeping, as I began developing this program, interviewing people, and designing and conducting workshops for people to explore ways to increase enjoyment in their work life and personal life.

Keeping a journal and rating what you do is an important part of the process. The journal will help you become more aware of what you are doing that you enjoy or don't enjoy, while the rating system will help you assess how much or how little you enjoy different things. It will also help you assess where you are starting from and then enable you to chart your progress as you work on upping your enjoyment.

Here are some tips on how to keep a journal and do these ratings.

Keeping Your Journal

Allow ten to twenty minutes at the end of each day, more if you feel so inspired, to write in your journal. Try to do this once a day, or at least every two or three days, if you are too busy to write every day. And realize that being too busy can be a sign you are working too hard and not allowing enough personal or enjoyment time in your life.

If you use a laptop or personal computer, you can use the Journal function in Microsoft Outlook and save it as an RTF file, which will provide a graphic display by date of these journal entries, along with your ratings. Or use any word processing program. Either way, label them by date with the year listed first, so you can easily retrieve them in order (i.e., 07-12-12 for December 12, 2007). You can print out these entries and keep them in a notebook for later review. Alternatively, use a notebook, preferably in a loose-leaf binder, and record your comments by hand.

As you reflect about the day, think about what you did in terms of how much you enjoyed different activities. The process is like keeping a diary, except that besides recording your activities, feelings, and observations, you also think about your level of enjoyment in participating in different activities and in inter-acting with different people. If you have trouble remembering what you did—more of a problem if you catch up with your journal after two or three days—use your daily calendar or date book as a reminder.

There are various ways to keep your journal. Use whichever approach or combination of approaches works best for you:

- Write up what happens chronologically.

- Focus on the activities and interactions you consider most important.

- Combine a series of routine activities into a single activity (such as: Made phone calls and wrote letters to follow up on a project)

- Separate activities according to whether they are work-related, personal activities, or both.

Start using the rating system with your journal as soon as possible. Just slip them in as you record different activities, events, or impressions with the numbers 0–10, where 5 is neu-tral. This will help you more quickly assess how you feel about what you did that day. And don't forget to give each day an overall rating at the end (i.e., overall, a 6 day).

At the end of the week, take five or ten minutes to review your entries for the week to see how you are doing. Notice any patterns or themes, such as activities or interactions you particu-larly enjoy and those you don't. Then, you can use the various techniques and games described in this book to decide what to do about these observations and make any desired changes. Make notes about your observations if you wish, and use this time to set goals or create a to-do list, which you can incorporate into your daily calendar or date book.

Every month, do a monthly review for twenty to thirty minutes. Again look for patterns or recurring themes, and note what actions you have taken to make changes (such as devoting an hour a day to engage in more activities you particularly enjoy) and what the results are.

Later, as you continue this process, you can set other milestones, such as a two-month and three-month review. After a time, when you are satisfied you have made the desired changes for increasing your enjoyment, you may find it unnecessary to continue keeping a journal and rating what you are doing. If so, put the process aside for a time and simply *enjoy!* Or if you enjoy keeping a journal and reflecting on what you have written, continue the process, noticing again and again how much you have upped your enjoyment.

Another way to use these journals (to be discussed in a later chapter) is to incorporate them into a regular discussion, support, and enjoyment games group. There you can share excerpts from your journals with each other and use what you have written to create fun role-play scenarios and visualizations to enact and experience what you would most like to do.

Rating Your Activities and Experiences

In rating your level of enjoyment, use a scale of 0–10 to express your feeling about an activity, from not liking it at all (0) to thinking that doing something or being with someone is the best (10). And if you feel neutral about an activity—you don't dislike doing it, but don't particularly enjoy doing it—use a 5.

When you make these ratings, put down the first number that comes to mind. Don't try to think about the process. Rather, let your intuitive, receptive mind give you a number and write it down. As you write in your journal, insert these numbers along with the entries; don't go back afterward to plug in the ratings numbers.

In addition to keeping a journal, you can keep a rating sheet to more graphically chart your day-to-day, weekly, and monthly process. To do so, list your activities or interactions on a calendar, which indicates the time devoted to that activity, followed by your rating. Then, you have an easy-to-review display for each day, and as you flip through it, you can readily see how you are doing. You can also use this ratings calendar to come up with overall ratings for different patterns you observe, as well as look at how you are doing at different times of the day. You can even come up with weighted averages based on how much time you are spending in different activities and how much you like participating in them, which might help you in spending less time on less enjoyable activities and devoting more time to activities you really enjoy.

For example, suppose you are spending an hour a day practicing your singing, which is something you really enjoy—rating it a 9, whereas you are spending three hours going to unnecessary meetings—which you rate at about a 3. So for those four hours, your average would be a 4.5—1 hour at 9 plus 3 hours at 3 ([9 + 9] ÷ 4 = 4.5). But if you can devote more time to your singing, say two hours, and cut down your unnecessary meetings to two hours that day, that would give you an average of 6 for that time period—2 hours at 9 plus 2 hours at 3 ([18 + 6] ÷ 4 = 6).

To calculate your final score for the day, add up the numbers in the final column (Total Score for Time Evaluated) and divide by the number of hours you evaluated that day. (Your computer's calculator will make this relatively painless.) In the case of the sales representative shown in the second chart, his total score was 86.5, and he evaluated 15 hours that day (on some other day, it might have been 14.5 hours, or 16 hours, for example). To simplify the math, round off to the nearest whole number.

Or forget about doing the math altogether. As you eyeball your Ratings Form for the day, you can see in general how you are spending your time and your ratings for that time period. Your goal should be to increase your ratings to 6 and up, and reduce the ratings of 5 and less as much as possible.

There's a rating form on the following page, followed by a sample form showing actual entries (from a sales manager) on an average workday.

As the sample form indicates, the salesman generally likes his job, but might want to reduce his time on phone calls, paperwork, and commuting or find ways to enjoy these activities more. Then there's that visit from Aunt Martha. Perhaps it's a family obligation, but maybe he and his wife could find a way to spend less time with her—or make her visit more enjoyable. The various techniques and games described in the next chapters can help him make the change.

So there you have it—the basic tools for beginning to assess where you are now and becoming more aware of where you are going.

The next chapters will help you review the barriers standing in the way of your enjoyment using a variety of techniques. As you get rid of or pass through these barriers, this progress will be reflected in your journal and your higher enjoyment rating scores.

So go to it. Start the process, have fun in applying the techniques, and *enjoy!*

Date of Entry:				
Time	Activity	Rating	Average for Time Evaluated	Total Score for Time Evaluated
8 am				
8:30				
9				
9:30				
10				
10:30				
11				
11:30				
12 pm				
12:30				
1				
1:30				
2				
2:30				
3				
3:30				
4				
4:30				
5				
5:30				
6				
6:30				
7				
7:30				
8				
8:30				
9				
9:30				
10				
10:30				
11				
11:30				
12 am				
Overall Rating for the Day: (Total Score from last column divided by # of hours in your day)				

			Average for	Total Score for
Time	Activity	Rating	Time Evaluated	Time Period
8 am	Get Up, breakfast	5		
8:30	Commute to work	3	4	8
9	Phone calls, paperwork	4		
9:30	"	4		
10	Sales meeting	6		
10:30	"	6	6	12
11	"	6		
11:30	Sales presentation	6		
12 pm	Lunch	8		
12:30	"	8		
1	"	8	8	20
1:30	"	8		
2	"	8		
2:30	Sales calls	6		
3	"	6		
3:30	"	6	6	15
4	"	6		
4:30	"	6		
5	Commute home (lots of traffic)	2	2	2
5:30	"	2		
6	Workout at gym	6		
6:30	"	6	7	14
7	Dinner	8		
7:30	"	8		
8	Watching TV	7	7	7
8:30	"	7		
9	Visit with Aunt Martha	2		
9:30	"	2	2	3
10	"	2		
10:30	Relax, nightcap with wife	8	8	8
11	"	8		
11:30				
12 am				
Overall Rating for the Day: (Total Score from last column divided by # of hours in your day)		5.93 (round to 6)		89

Date of Entry: January 1, 2007

5

Silence Your Inner Critical Voice

For many people, the inner critical voice can be a big barrier to enjoyment. This is the voice that has messages like "work harder," "don't waste time," "do what everyone else is doing," or "do what's practical; don't pursue unrealistic dreams." It's a voice that can keep you working diligently at what you don't want to do or need to do, while keeping you from doing what you enjoy. Or if you do what you enjoy, it will leave you feeling guilty or fretful about what you aren't doing, so you don't enjoy doing it after all. Thus, this inner critical voice can be as hard a taskmaster as the voice of your conscience or superego.

The Voice of Judgment

Michael Ray and Rochelle Myers call this critical inner voice the "Voice of Judgment" or "VOJ" in their classic book, *Creativity in Business*.[1] It is the voice of fear, anxiety, and critical judgment that knocks down new ideas, blocks risk-taking, and can stand in the way of relaxing and having fun. As they observe: "This judgment condemns, criticizes, attaches blame, makes fun of, puts down, assigns guilt, passes sentence on, punishes, and buries anything that's the least bit unlike a mythical norm."[2]

They identify four different types of negative judgment: self-judgment, judgment from others, collective judgment, and judging the judgment.[3]

Self-judgment is your inner critical voice that speaks to you as a parent, teacher, cop, or other authority figure putting up strictures and restrictions for what is the correct, moral, and responsible behavior. But unfortunately, these rules can continue to weigh you down, even after circumstances have changed and so have some of the rules. And many of these judgments can act like stoplights that keep you from doing something you would enjoy or that prevent you from enjoying it. For instance, the voice echoing in your head might tell you: "Don't waste time," "Don't spend time in frivolous activities," "That's foolish," "Don't make a fool of yourself," and the like. You hold yourself back if you listen to that voice.

The *judgment from others* essentially acts to confirm your own Voice of Judgment and therefore seems like a confirming truth. Or as Ray and Myers explain: "This kind of external judgment . . . gets its power from your confirming internal judgment. Less obviously, it also gets its original impetus from your own VOJ: You send out signals, and someone else picks them up and speaks them aloud as facts."[4] For example, a significant other echoes what your Voice of Judgment is already saying to you, such as "Don't waste time by going to that party; you have important work to do." So as much as you might want to take a fun break (and can in fact afford the time), the words of the other person, coupled with your own feelings of hesitation that he or she might have picked up, hold you back.

The *collective judgment* represents the voice of your culture speaking to you in the form of fashion, national and cultural preferences, social class expectations, and everyday etiquette. While such norms or rules for behavior can be a handy guide for what to do, it is also an external behavior standard, and you should still feel free to choose how to behave. Yes, it often helps to go along with this collective voice; but at times, it can stifle your creativity and ability to enjoy things you otherwise would. For example, you would love to be an actor or performer, whether as a career choice or in a local amateur theater group, but your family or relatives say no, it's not a respectable calling.

Finally, the fourth level of judgment whereby you *judge the judgment* comes into play when you feel bad for trying to put aside one of the other levels of judgment. Then, you feel bad for feeling bad, which occurs because your "judgment judges the judgment and lays the blame on you."[5]

In sum, your VOJ, which takes the form of your own thinking or self-talk to yourself, comes from a number of sources— parents, teachers, family members, friends, religious leaders, business associates, and your culture and society as a whole. But whatever its source or combination of sources, it can hold you back from acting freely, including doing things you enjoy, because your VOJ shouts "No!"

Thinking About Your Own Critical Voice

A good example of how this critical voice can interfere with doing something enjoyable is what happened to Jack, who was brought up in an upper-middle-class professional family, where his parents and close relatives were filled with doctors, lawyers, and high-level management professionals. Thus, he grew up with an expectation that he would follow a similar career path, and he took the kind of preparatory classes in college that would lead to such a career.

Then, he took some time out between graduation and going to graduate school to gain management experience in one of the family businesses. But he had long felt conflicted about taking any of these career paths—one reason he had put off going to grad school until his mid-twenties was that he was intrigued by reading about discoveries of ancient Indian burial grounds and was drawn to becoming an archaeologist. Yet he felt torn because from his family's perspective, which he had internalized, an archaeologist seemed like a glorified construction worker or gravedigger, not at all up to family standards. So for months, as he kept postponing grad school, he struggled over what to do: his critical voice kept telling him: "Become a lawyer or get an MBA," while his passion was for traveling the world as an archaeologist.

Eventually, he gave in to his critical voice, with the prodding of his parents echoing and confirming that as the most practical choice, so for a time he did enroll in law school. But after a year he was so miserable and felt so much turmoil, that he finally decided to drop out, helped in part by a support group for law school students who didn't want to be lawyers. Then, with his parents finally coming to recognize that he would never be successful or happy as a lawyer, they finally came around to supporting his decision to go to grad school to become an archaeologist, which he did, finally feeling he had responded to his true calling.

The same kind of critical voice can similarly hold you back from making personal choices you otherwise would like to make, such as when you want to choose friends or a mate from outside your "acceptable" choices but say no because of your critical judgment. And likewise this voice can keep you from engaging in social activities, selecting colors for your home or office, going on trips, making purchases, or making other choices outside of your ordinary zone of what's usual and expected in your life. In a sense, this critical voice is keeping you confined and restricted, so your choices are more limited. In some cases, these choices may be wise ones to keep you safe, but in many cases they can be holding you back from being more creative and experiencing success in ways that would be fun and enjoyable for you.

So take some time to think about your own critical voice. The first step to taking control of it and destroying these negative restrictive thoughts, fears, and feelings of guilt that make up this voice is to become aware of when your critical voice kicks in. You want to notice when you have negative and judgmental thoughts. According to Ray and Myers, you want to first notice when this judgment is present and then identify precisely what it is saying by listening to that voice within.[6]

A good way to do this is to keep a little notebook with you, so you can write down whenever you have a judgmental thought. You should also be especially alert for this inner voice when you feel fearful, anxious, or depressed about something. (If it's not convenient to write down a note, such as during a meeting or conversation, while driving, or while listening to a lecture, mentally keep track until you have the chance to record it.)

Besides keeping count, notice what the critical voice is saying to you, whatever form it takes, from a quiet commentary to a sad observation to an angry remark. For instance, you might hear your voice saying something like: "You've made a mistake again; you're never going to get it right" or "You loser; why did you think he/she would say yes?" You might even keep a Critical Voice Journal to keep track of the type of negative judgments you keep making.

Then, take some time each day to reflect on the statements of your critical voice. Notice the types of statements that are most common and in what type of situations they most often occur, such as at work or in your personal life. Notice not only when you judge yourself but when you listen to and accept the judgments. Also, note if this voice has prevented you from doing something in the past or recently or if it might be interfering in any of your plans for the future.

You can use the chart on the following page to help you notice these patterns.

What Is My Critical Voice Telling Me?			
Statements of My Critical Voice	Common Themes	When Has My Critical Voice Prevented Me from Doing Something	What Might My Critical Voice Prevent Me from Doing in the Future

Next, after you have taken some time to become aware of your voice, whether you record your thoughts in a journal or not, Ray and Myers recommend using a kind of meditation called "witness consciousness" or the "observing self," where you remind yourself that you are not your thoughts but you are your inner self or essence.[7] This way, you affirm that you are not this critical voice or VOJ that is chattering in your mind.

Getting Rid of Your Critical Voice

Once you have become aware of your critical voice, you can control it so you can listen to it when you feel it is making sense and being practical and get rid of it when you feel it is putting you down and putting blocks in the path of your success and enjoyment. Here are some various strategies to use.

- *Decide if this is a helpful practical warning to listen to; if not, use the strategies listed below to get rid of it.* Here you want to look to your reason or intuition to help you decide if the reason makes sense as a helpful warning, or if it is just coming from your irrational fears and anxieties. To this end, you might have a discussion with yourself where you reflect on what your critical voice is saying and argue against it; then decide which approach makes the most sense. Or alternatively, imagine you are looking at the statement on your mental screen and call on your intuition, which comes from your inner essence to tell you yea or nay. Sometimes you will find your critical voice does have a useful caution and is worth considering and listening to; but commonly, it is more the Voice of Judgment putting the kibosh on something that is worthwhile or enjoyable for you to do.

- *Fight back against your critical voice.* Once you have decided your critical voice is not helping with a given situation, attack it in your imagination or physically act out this confrontation. For example, talk back to it with a firm, stern message, such as: "Go away. I don't want you in my life now." And then if your critical voice argues back, with a statement like: "But you know you can make more money if you choose that career, even if you would rather do something else," restate your position with even more firmness, even anger, such as: "No, I don't want to listen to you. Leave me alone." And for even further emphasis, you might state your position out loud, even yell at your critical voice. (Do this when you are alone, please. You don't want people around you thinking you are nuts.) Perhaps even stomp your

foot or bring down your arm for further emphasis. You'll find
as you repeat this process, you'll become firmer and
stronger—and when you confront your critical voice on another issue, you'll be stronger and more confident, too. The
process is the same for overcoming any foe—a previous experience of being successful will help you gain strength for
the next time you confront that enemy again.

• *Make your critical judgment seem ridiculous.* Another suggestion
for squelching your critical voice, proposed by Ray and
Myers, is to find a way to make this judgment look ridiculous, such as by blowing it up like a balloon until it bursts.[8]
To do so, close your eyes and imagine you are hearing the
statement of your critical voice or seeing it in your mind's
eye. Then, imagine that this statement is becoming larger
and larger, even in flashing lights or booming out from an
echo chamber. Or you might even see the words projected in
large letters on the top of a mountain, like the Hollywood
Hills sign. Then, imagine the statement becoming so huge
that it actually bursts, and as it does, laugh mentally or out
loud at the pitiful ridiculousness of this statement that you
have been able to destroy so easily.

• *Use your curiosity to overcome the critical voice.* In this approach,
you think back to when you had the curiosity of a child and
experience the sense of wonder and enthusiasm you had
then for exploring and trying new things. So then, when you
hear your critical voice rearing its ugly head to put you down
or belittle something you want to do, call on that essential
curiosity you had as a child to question what the critical
voice is telling you now. As Ray and Myers point out: "Remember that the VOJ is a criticism. Its function is to close
the door on further investigation or even curiosity; like a
flashbulb, it reveals its all in one brief burst."[9] But instead,
you respond with a critique to illuminate what the critical

voice is saying to you, so you can combat whatever it is saying that is wrong or misleading. Or as Ray and Myers put it:
"The character of the VOJ is to put you down and keep you
there; the character of your own objective intelligence and
curiosity is to open you up to new experiences and satisfaction."[10]

• *Use meditation to get rid of your critical voice.* Another approach
to still your judgmental voice is to get very relaxed and focus
on a very positive thought, word, or sound. Then, in the stillness, remain focused on that thought, and any time a critical
idea comes to you, say to yourself quietly, "Go away," and
then refocus back on the positive thought, word, or sound.
Click your thumb and index finger together if you like to
create a trigger association with that (or if you already use
this trigger for something else, use another small move-
ment). This process of repeatedly sending your judgment
away will help to build up a habit that will carry over to
other times when these critical thoughts come to you. Just
say "Go away" to yourself or use your trigger association to
stop the critical voice from speaking to you.

• *Use physical exercise to still your critical voice.* Physical exercise
can also help eliminate your critical voice by helping you
unwind and shifting your attention to other things. This is a
particularly good way to stop feelings of fear, anxiety, and
depression that are often associated with an influx of critical
judgments about yourself that put you down and sap your
confidence. But if you do something physical, such as running, swimming, or cycling, and concentrate on that exercise, so you are in the moment, you stop the flow of
judgmental thoughts. (You will also feel good about having
done something to increase your energy level!)

• *Use the "But Why" technique if you have a stated goal but haven't
been able to reach it despite some effort to do so.* In this approach,

also suggested by Myers and Ray, you try to uncover the reason that some judgment or fear is blocking your way and keeping you from doing what you really want to do and achieving your stated goal.[11] They suggest doing this with a partner, where you ask each other "what's stopping you?" and write down your answers. Then you exchange sheets and ask the other person to determine what is going on based on the answers. But you can also do it yourself. Just be open and honest as you probe for reasons. Start by writing down the goal you haven't been able to reach, such as: "I want to do work that is really meaningful to me" at the top of the page. Or note down something you would enjoy doing but have been held back from doing by your judgments and fears. Then, make a list of all your but's. Just write down whatever comes to mind as a reason you haven't been able to reach your goal, such as: "But I'm afraid I'm not good enough," "But I don't want to risk leaving my current job," "But I fear I'll be rejected again if I try," and so on. After you list all your blocks, notice how your excuses are triggered by your critical judgments and fears. Then, think about whether those concerns are truly realistic, which means you need to set another goal. Or if you really do want to reach your goal, you can use some of the techniques described in this chapter for getting rid of those judgments and fears. You can use the chart on the following page for creating your list. So there you have it—the basic steps to identifying and getting rid of your critical judgments and fears standing in the way of achieving what you want or enjoying what you want to do. Now it's up to you. Start with something you want to achieve or enjoy but haven't been able to in the past and start identifying and sending those blocks and barriers away.

Reasons for Not Achieving My Goal or Doing Something I Would Enjoy Doing

My Goal Is:

Why I Haven't Achieved My Goal or Done Something I Want to Do	How Realistic Is This Block? (from 1–5)	Can I Overcome This Block? How?
But . . .		
But . . .		
But . . .		
But . . .		
But . . .		
But . . .		
But . . .		
But . . .		
But . . .		

6

Rediscover Your Inner Child

Besides getting rid of your inner critic, rediscovering your inner child can help to unleash feelings of enjoyment, as well as increased creativity. Your inner kid is characterized by playfulness, spontaneity, enthusiasm, curiosity, an interest in learning, and a spirit of intuition. These qualities often get tamped down by society in the form of parents, teachers, and other authority figures, since the ideal is to be rational, control your impulses, and conform. Certainly you need these latter traits to get along with others and thrive in modern society. But you need the other qualities, too, for balance, and they bring vitality into your life.

As play expert Johan Huizinga describes in *Homo Ludens,* the play activity of children is characterized by an intensity, absorption, spirit of fun, and use of the imagination, which helps to create an alternate play world.[1] It is a nonserious, voluntary activity that involves stepping out of real life into a temporary other reality, and it adds pleasure to everyday life. As Huizinga puts it: "[Play] adorns life, amplifies it, and is to that extent a necessity both for the individual—as a life function—and for society . . ."[2]

Where Did My Inner Child Go?

However, in the process of being socialized, these childlike qualities are often squelched, or the pressures of everyday life and
feelings of obligation may drive that spirit of fun from your life,
as the following stories illustrate. So along with banishing your
inner critic, you need to bring back your inner kid, so you can
call on it to increase your enjoyment in life.

Following are examples of three people I interviewed who
need to find their inner kid.

An Overworked Magazine Editor

Erin is a magazine editor who felt overworked and burned out
after a series of jobs at small publications. On each job, she mi-
cromanaged the work, since she didn't trust the writers she
hired; often, after several rewrites, she would rewrite the material herself. As a result, deadlines were repeatedly nearly missed,
and Erin often had screaming fights with writers defending their
work or protesting her demands, leading to high turnover. After
a year or two of this, Erin would be fired or leave in frustration
and move on to the next job, where the pattern repeated itself
again and again.

Erin's work style, in turn, undermined her health. Though
she was only in her thirties, she already had ulcers and high
blood pressure, and her *joie de vivre* and spirit of adventure were
gone. In the beginning, she had really enjoyed the work, especially the variety of tasks and the different subjects she learned
about every day. But now, the tension buildup had turned her
into a kind of steam engine, which boiled over from time to time,
spewing her anger outward to others and inward to herself.

Erin was desperately in need of a fun-makeover. She needed
to learn to lighten up, and bring back the spirit of relaxation and
joy to her work to help both herself and her downtrodden
staffers.

An Engineer Who Worked Too Long and Hard

Similarly, Jerry could benefit greatly from getting reacquainted with his inner kid. As an engineer, he often worked long hours both at work and at home doing detailed, mostly solitary work, allowing little time for relaxation and play. Unlike Erin, he didn't yell or scream at anyone, but he tended to be withdrawn and shy. As a little kid, he had enjoyed many games, from playing tag and volleyball to board games and video games. But he had long ago left such interests behind, and now lived a bland, colorless life, with a lack of highs and lows. Sometimes he felt bored or empty, but mostly he went through life in a neutral state, where he did his work responsibly, with his emotions cut off, so he felt neither satisfied nor dissatisfied, yet wasn't really fulfilled or happy.

A Frenetic, Harried Housewife

Harriet is an example of a frenetic, harried housewife, much in need of a reconnection with her inner child. While her attorney husband went to work, she worked a few hours a day as an elementary school teacher, and barreled through the rest of the day doing errands and chores and shuttling her kids around to classes and extracurricular activities. She experienced little fun in life, viewing her days mostly as getting through one activity after another. Even visiting relatives was more a chore than enjoyment, since when she visited her two brothers and their families with her husband and two kids, her brothers would generally be glued to the TV set, watching some game. Then, while she and the other adults sat in the living room watching TV, and the kids went off to play in their rooms or the backyard, she would count the minutes until they could leave. Later, when she and her family got back home, there were more chores to do. So life for Harriet was a blur of not particularly enjoyable activities. She didn't know how to relax and have fun; she desperately needed to recapture the spirit of joy she once had as a young child.

Three Ways to Rediscover Your Inner Kid

So how do you find and bring out your inner kid? The three major ways are these:

1. *Reflect back to the times when you really enjoyed yourself as a child and re-experience those times again. Or reflect back to your idealized vision of childhood.* This process is also useful for remembering the activities that you really enjoyed and might want to pursue again, as described in Part IV.

2. *Imagine you are a kid again—you pick the age—as you participate in a variety of activities in the here and now.* First, use this approach in a series of trials or role-plays to get familiar with the process. Then apply it to other activities to enjoy whatever you are doing more, such as going to a social networking event that might otherwise seem routine; doing daily tasks that might normally seem dull; or going to a brainstorming meeting to help you generate ideas.

3. *Participate in events designed to bring out the kid in you,* such as the Recess event described later in this chapter, which was designed to help adults relax and enjoy like children.

The following exercises and games will help you put these different approaches into action.

Recapture Your Inner Kid by Reflecting Back to Childhood

Your memory or imagination is a way to tap into your inner kid. If you have great memories of childhood, use your own recollections. If you associate your childhood more with difficult times than with good times, imagine what it would be like to be your ideal image of a child, with ideal parents, in an ideal home, and use that image, since this purpose of this process is to think about the positive qualities you associate with childhood.

One way to recall these positive past memories is to use positive words you associate with childhood. Another method is to get relaxed, in a quiet, meditative state and remember back. A third is to go on a guided fantasy/journey into being a child again. Following are these three different techniques. Use the technique or techniques that you like best and try experimenting with them at different times.

Word Power

Pick an age from early childhood (between ages five and seven), another from your middle childhood years (between eight and eleven), and another from your early teens (between twelve and fourteen). Then, thinking back to each time period, think of as many positive associations as you have for yourself or for children in general of that age. For example, some qualities that may come to mind include: creativity, spontaneity, excitement, enthusiasm, curiosity, and so on.

Keep brainstorming for a couple of minutes or until the qualities stop coming to you. Should you recall any qualities you consider negative (i.e., impulsiveness), put those aside, let them go, and bring your attention back to brainstorming about positive qualities.

Next, take a few minutes to look at the list of qualities you have come up with. Say the words over and over to yourself, prefacing them by the words: "I am," (i.e., "I am curious," "I am enthusiastic," "I am joyful.") If you have a long list (ten or more words), pick out your seven favorite words to use in the exercise. Then, as you say each word, see yourself as this younger version of you or as your idealized kid experiencing this quality. In your mind's eye, experience yourself acting out a situation where you express this quality.

For example, if the quality that comes to mind is "curiosity," you might imagine yourself individually or with some children of your selected age group expressing curiosity. Some possibilities might be exploring a cave together, reading an exciting book about adventure travel, or learning about a new type of dinosaur in science class. Or suppose one of your words is "creativity." Imagine doing whatever you think is creative and fun at the age you selected, such as rearranging colored blocks to build an unusual-looking house at age five or acting in a school play at age eight.

You can use the chart on the following page to write down and reflect on the different words you come up with.

The Positive Qualities Kids Have (mark your favorite words with *)		
Age 5–7	Age 8–11	Age 12–14

Remember When

In this technique, you will think back to different times when you experienced really fun, exciting things. Preferably, recall experiences from your own childhood. If they don't readily come to mind, imagine yourself as a child having these experiences— either as yourself or as your ideal image of a child.

To start the process, get in a relaxed, comfortable state in a quiet place by yourself or with a group of people who are participating in the process. Then, imagine you are between five and seven years old, and you are doing something you enjoy very much, say going to a friend's birthday party, enjoying a ride in an amusement park, watching a circus performance, paddling in the waves of a beach, or eating delicious cotton candy. Whatever it is, you're experiencing it on a beautiful sunny day, alone or with your friends or family, and you are having a wonderful time.

Continue to go where that experience takes you, and at any time you experience anything negative or scary, turn away from that image, let it go, and replace it with something fun and enjoyable. The point of this journey into your imagination is to highlight what you really like doing, so you can experience the fun of being a carefree, imaginative, happy kid again—whether you are re-experiencing a real experience or creating an imaginary scenario in your mind.

After a few minutes or when that experience feels complete, go on to the next phase of childhood, when you are between eight and eleven years old. Again, imagine you are doing something you enjoy very much, whether you really did this as a child or are imagining the experience, such as having a picnic, taking a hike, going on your first airplane ride, racing on your bike, or whatever you really enjoy. Take a few minutes to feel you are there and enjoy the experience.

Next, after a few minutes or when that experience feels complete, go to your early teenage years, from about twelve to four-teen years old. Once more, see yourself doing something you find very enjoyable, whether you did this in the past or are imag-ining it now, such as sailing or windsurfing, going on a camping trip, skiing down a mountain side, or going horseback riding.

After a few minutes of savoring the experience or when the experience feels complete, let go of that experience, and gradu-ally, return to the present by counting backwards from 5 to 1, and come back into the room.

Take some time to notice what happened during your experi-ence, so you can incorporate what you have learned from it into the here and now. Some things to notice and questions to ask to guide your observations are these:

- How did you feel about being a kid again? (If you found any difficulty getting into the experience, try again. It may take some time and practice to tap into that childlike state of being.)

- What did you most enjoy doing? What did you find espe-cially enjoyable about doing this?

- How can you apply that experience to your everyday life now? Are these activities you might like to do again now? Or can you incorporate the attitude to life you experienced into making choices about what you are doing or how you are doing it now?

Creating Fun Fantasies of Being a Kid

Another way to tap into your inner kid is to imagine yourself engaging in fantasy adventures as a kid. The process is like going to the movies, except that you are in the movie creating your own adventure story. You are not just watching someone else on the movie screen as a detached observer. Rather, you are a participant in the adventure. Later, through practice, you can transfer this same spirit of creativity, fantasy, and adventure into your everyday experiences and perk up your day. For example, say you are waiting on a long line when you are shopping or stuck in traffic or have a long wait at the airport. You can project yourself into your own fantasy adventure and let your mind soar.

Initially, when you use this technique, get relaxed and close your eyes to more fully project yourself into the experience. But in time, with practice, you can learn to do this with your eyes open, so you can trigger such an experience anywhere. This approach is also a great tool for increasing your creativity generally, such as in brainstorming new ideas—and best of all, it's fun.

Following is an example of a guided fantasy. Here's how to start using this fun fantasy technique:

- Read the fantasy to yourself as a general guide to trigger your own fantasy adventure.

- Record the fantasy guide into a tape recorder, and play it back, while you go on the adventure.

- Get together with a friend or group. Have one person read the fantasy guide aloud while the rest experience the adventure.

Once you have a general idea of how the process works, create your own fantasy adventures, so you can go wherever you want in your mind, as a kid of whatever age you choose.

The following journey is adapted from my book *Mind Power*[3] in a chapter entitled "Use the Power of Your Mind to Get Away From It All." That's exactly what you are doing in imagining yourself as a kid.

Before you start the process, imagine yourself at any age from five to fourteen and imagine you are going on the journey yourself or are with a companion or group of friends. As you experience a number of these trips, you might notice differences in the experience at different ages and whether you are alone or with others. If so, compare and contrast them, and notice which age or type of journey you prefer. For example, did you feel freer and more spontaneous as a young child or as a teenager? Did you prefer journeying on your own or with others? Eventually, you may find that you like choosing a particular age or setting to go on these fantasies. Or perhaps you might prefer experimenting, trying out ages and types of journeys. Do whatever feels more fun and interesting for you.

Blast Off for a Journey to Outer Space

Kids of all ages are fascinated by space travel; so here's a chance to become a kid again as you take off into space.

> You are on an orbiting space station, about to become a passenger on a spaceship voyaging far beyond our galaxy to an intergalactic space community on a faraway planet. It is the year 3000.
>
> Now enter the space ship. Go directly to your life-support capsule. It is very comfortable inside and you can relax completely, as you travel to a distant galaxy. As you get ready to take off, think about how fun and exciting this is going to be.
>
> Now feel the ship sway slightly as it blasts off from planet Earth. As it does, look out of the small window next to your capsule and see Earth falling away below you. Soon it begins to look like a small ball, with patches of green and blue representing the continents and the oceans.
>
> Glance about and notice the vast black expanse of space before you; here and there you see clusters of stars twinkling brightly. You feel a great sense of curiosity and enthusiasm, excited by this chance to explore new worlds. All you can hear is the whirr of the spacecraft, and beyond that, only silence everywhere.
>
> Now, to experience the weightlessness of space, put on your spacesuit and leave your life-support capsule for a few minutes. Attach your

lifeline and open the hatch. As you step out into space, feel yourself floating. You feel weightless, suspended on a vast inky sea, filled with sparkling white dots.

It's time to return to the ship. Your destination is approaching fast, for while you have been floating, your ship has been hurtling through thousands of miles of space, so fast and smoothly you haven't noticed. So get back into your life-support capsule, as your ship comes to the end of your journey.

Now notice a large planet before you. It is made up of grey granite rocks and soil; and you can see jagged crags and wide plateaus rising above the surface. On one plateau, you notice a long white air strip. Your spaceship is heading toward this. As the ship comes closer, it slows down, until finally it lands gently on the center of the strip.

Go to the hatchway, push it open, and step out. After you comes the captain of the ship, whom you haven't seen before. He is tall, rugged-looking, wearing a white spacesuit like yours. He motions to tell you it is safe to explore wherever you want. So you wander off feeling safe, confident, and eager to explore.

You first approach an unusual rock formation that intrigues you. It is tall, shaped like a lightning bolt, and you walk around it looking at all the shapes and angles.

Then, as you walk on, you pass small mossy plants clinging to the rocks. Pick one up. It looks soft, mossy, and you can rub your hands over it, as if you are playing with clay.

Next, you pass a few oddly shaped boulders. They are round, but with a series of ridges and projections. Strangely, they feel light when you lift them. When you drop them, they bounce slightly a few times. You can try throwing them around as if you are playing ball. If you have a companion with you, try playing catch.

After a while, you approach the outskirts of a settlement. There are a few houses, buildings, and free-standing walls. But, they are different from any structures you have seen on earth, as a series of projections jut out from each surface. Curious, you go over and explore these closely.

Then, in the distance, you notice a few humanoids riding toward you in an open jeep-like vehicle. There are three of them, and they appear very different from people on earth. They have large round heads, small eyes, long gangly arms, and are wearing silvery metallic suits. But they seem friendly. As they pull up toward you, they motion you over and offer you a ride to see their city.

You get in, and, as you drive, they tell you about some of their customs—what their family life is like, about their government, how they make a living. Listen as they describe their way of life. (How clever of you to have worn your universal translator.)

Now you enter their city center. It is made up of large domed houses built from strange white rocks with long projections. The small domes are private houses; the larger ones apartment buildings; the very biggest, government and cultural buildings. Take some time to explore. You can visit some people in their homes if you like and see how they live.

You hear a loud whine coming from the vehicle. Your hosts are motioning to you to tell you it's time to go back to your ship. You return to their vehicle, and they drive you back. There you shake hands to say goodbye and re-enter your ship. Inside you get back in your life-support capsule, take off your spacesuit, and drift off to sleep, dreaming about the planet you have seen. When you awake, your ship is landing at Earth's space station again. Refreshed, you get up and leave your vessel. Once again you are home.

On a subsequent trip, you can create your own planetary world and space beings.

Now that you have the general idea for taking fantasy trips, you can create your own. Just imagine the experiences kids would like to have at different ages, or draw on your memories to create a fantasy adventure in your mind. Imagine yourself as a kid in a time machine going back to become a part of any period in history. Or imagine yourself taking part in an exciting, adventurous sport, like skydiving or sports car racing, or going on safari or diving for sunken treasure.

Just decide where to go and let your receptive, intuitive mind sweep you along. You can go on your own or go on a group fantasy, where one person leads the group by describing aloud what he or she sees while on the trip. You can alternate leading the group, much like the game of "continue the story" that kids play, taking turns adding to the story.

You can also turn these fantasy adventures into a special occasion to make the experience even more dramatic and set off from everyday reality. To do so, light a few candles and dim the lights; put on some music that fits the mood of the trip, such as fast, lively music if you are going to a circus or amusement park; spacey, dramatic music if you are taking an outer space or underwater trip.

Imagine You Are a Kid Again in the Here and Now

Another approach to bringing out your inner kid is to imagine you are a kid as you participate in everyday activities. Don't try these exercises at work when you are doing something critical and need all your adult powers to operate successfully, such as making a presentation or meeting with a client. But if you are doing routine, tedious tasks, imagining that you are doing them as a kid can add a sparkle to your day.

A good way to get started is with a few trial runs. Say you are taking a jog around your neighborhood or walking the dog. Imagine that you are a younger you—say in elementary school or junior high. Then look around at what you see as that kid.

For example, suppose builders are renovating an old house in your neighborhood. As the normal you, you might just walk by, making a mental note that the Joneses are getting a paint job and fixing their garage. But as a young kid, you stop and are curious to learn more. So walk up to the house, and if you can, walk around it. Peek in the windows. Imagine what the house will be like when the construction is completed and it is furnished inside.

Or suppose you are jogging around the park for your daily

exercise. Usually you might listen to music through headphones on your iPod. But now, to become a kid again, turn the player off, or better yet, don't bring it, so you don't have to carry it. Then, as you jog, think of yourself as a kid again; say you are nine or ten. Just thinking about this, you'll likely experience more energy and run faster. As you run, pay particular attention to any kids you see and notice what they are doing. Observe how they are running around, exploring, being very curious, and do the same. For instance, if the kids are playing in a playground, stop to watch and imagine yourself swinging on the swings, digging in the dirt, playing tag with another child. If there is a pond with ducks, stop to watch; point at them and wave; perhaps call out to them by playfully quacking.

After you have experimented with being a kid on your own to try out the process, try being a kid in everyday activities. For example, when you go shopping, imagine you are going into the store as a kid. Then, as you look around, notice that you are more curious and everything seems newer and more vibrant, for you are seeing the everyday world with the greater curiosity, playfulness, and spontaneity of a kid. You may also find when you put on your kid persona that the people you interact with, such as a store clerk, are friendlier, livelier, cheerier, because they pick up your childlike spirit. That way, the exchange becomes more fun.

So experiment, enjoy. And if you can, compare notes with others who are experimenting with being a kid. You'll get other ideas for applying the process, as well as affirmation and support for what you are doing.

Participate in Events to Bring Out the Kid in You

Finally, you may find events in your area designed to bring out your inner kid. If so, go participate in them and enjoy.

One such group is Playfair, which uses fun and humor to

promote teambuilding at work. The organization was founded by Matt Weinstein in 1975. I went to some of their events in San Francisco in the late 1970s, when these occasions were like social mixers that involved play activities for between fifty and a hundred people, though now the company focuses on putting on corporate presentations and events.

Another play for adults group, which used to be called Recess for Adults, founded by Sue Walden, who now runs a theater arts organization called ImprovWorks, was devoted to promoting learning skills through improvisation. The company offered performances, public classes, and workshops in which people of all ages were invited to "explore the joy and power of improvisation." (ImprovWorks still offers Recess! Play Nights for Grown-Ups, which are described on their website at www.improvworks .org as "a laugh-filled evening of fun and games to build relationship skills, including getting acquainted processes, communication games, and how to stay open and appreciative of differences.") I went to one of these events some years ago, which I described in *Fantasy Worlds*.[4] Here's an excerpt, adapted to illustrate how such events with others can tap into your playful child.

> The Recess for Adults program put on by Sue Walden & Company, an organization devoted to improvisation training, was based on using improvisation. It's a technique in which a person spontaneously reacts to, invents, or creates a spur-of-the-moment response—in words, gestures, actions, or by creating a brief minidrama. Often the improv involves fantasy, because as a person responds in these ways, he or she often taps into that playful inner child, lets it out, and becomes like a kid again, acting without the usual thinking about what he or she is doing. Also, in an improv, a person sometimes takes on the character of another person; imagines himself or herself as an object, animal, or plant; or tells or enacts an invented story.

The event is called "Recess" to highlight the playful escape from the everyday world to a world of fun.

The Recess night I attended was an evening of such improv activities put on in a large dance studio–like room. To help everyone step even more into this other reality, Sue had one important rule—no mention of real-world jobs or occupations. She even had a warning on the blackboard: the word "jobs" was written inside a circle, with a big slash through it. The reason for this taboo was that we unconsciously make assumptions about people based on their occupations; also, jobs are down-to-earth, real-world, practical things, while this was an evening about playing, letting out the child within.

Indeed, just about anything that roots us in specific present-day reality can be a barrier to fantasy and play, since our everyday roles—whether in a job or as a parent or member of a church or social group—has certain expectations and usual behaviors and practices associated with it. Jobs are one of the most defining. To the degree we act in keeping with these expectations, we are held by the boundaries of this reality. In contrast, by engaging in play and letting out the child within, we let go of these ordinary expectations and behaviors to imagine and enact new possibilities. While it is certainly possible to imagine other ways to enact these everyday roles or imagine new roles replacing them (such as if a judge were to suddenly step out of character to sing an instruction to the jury, which responds with a chorus), normally we think about and are guided by our roles and those of others, and that prevents us from using a playful or imaginative approach to explore new roles and relate in new ways. Thus, disconnecting us from job roles contributed to this process of unlinking from present-day reality to be more receptive to the possibilities for fantasy and play.

Once it was time to start, we sat down in the circle of chairs in the center of the room, and Sue stepped in the center of the group. She began by explaining the kinds of things we would be doing that would contribute to the fantasy of being

a kid again, such as learning to let go, relax, and be spontaneous.

Such activities can trigger the fantasy process, along with
evoking past memories of childhood. Another key to moving
into the childlike state of mind is letting go of the logical, linear thinking part of the mind, because this helps us become
more spontaneous and experience sensations more directly. It
is this same letting go of logical, linear thinking that contributes to fantasy, creativity, and playfulness, so anything that
encourages the one, encourages the other. This is because
thinking that is centered in the left hemisphere of the brain is
analytical. This logical style of thinking sees things in a se-
quenced, orderly way, like an analog computer, and focuses on
what it is. It is objective and real-world oriented.

For example, one exercise helped us let go of this logical
mind by getting us to act without thinking by responding on
a physical, visceral level. To help us get into this state, Sue
instructed: "Just call out a way to move, the name of any body
part, and a category."

And that's what happened. Soon people were crawling,
skipping, jumping, hopping on one leg around the room. They
were waving arms, wiggling toes, swinging knees, and yelling
out words like "rutabagas, bananas, peaches, kiwifruit, pears,
apples." Later, in discussing the experience, people described
how they felt a sense of letting go. They responded more directly and automatically, much like a stimulus-and-response
reaction, and they felt a freeing of their emotions. Such more
immediate responses are linked to this more intuitive, image-
making, metaphor-creating part of our mind that is most inti-
mately involved with creating fantasies. The ability to act like
a child again can help us access that by freeing us from our
controlling and analytical logical mind.

Chase-and-capture games are another classic activity of
the childhood play spirit, and the next few games reflected
this excitement. The first of these involved a key element
sometimes included in fantasy play—using one thing to sym-

bolize something else. For example, a stick becomes not just a stick, but a magic wand. A stone becomes not just a stone, but a place of mystery and power.

After Recess, we had refreshments before going home. It was a time of transition out of the fantasy world of the evening and into everyday reality, as the rules suspended for the event to let out the little child in us were put back in place. People began to talk about everyday, ordinary activities—even jobs.

This gradual transformation back to everyday rules and roles highlighted how this evening had been transformed into an alternate reality through letting out the inner child. There had been a shared permission to play games, be spontaneous, be creative, and otherwise act like a child again. Moreover, the activities we engaged in re-created many of the types of play most of us experienced as children. These games also encouraged immediate physical and intuitive responses, which helped us push aside the more usual rational, analytical, thinking adult part of ourselves. While everyday life was like being in school and following the rules of the classroom, this was recess, where everyone was encouraged to play like a child, without the usual restrictions of the adult world.

For some people, this sense of openness and spontaneity was also a way to meet others, besides having fun, since this atmosphere helped to open up the usual barriers to conversation, and the shared experience created a sense of rapport that helped the meeting process, too.

As this description illustrates, this experience of learning to play again like a child can be brought out in a group session, where everyone has permission to act like a child. The activity can be a great deal of fun as a chance to get out of adult roles and responsibilities to re-experience the spontaneity, freedom, creativity, and excitement of the child. Then, having this experience, you can take that with you into your everyday life, and as appropriate, call on that inner playful kid to bring more fun into your life.

7

Eliminate Other Enjoyment Blocks

Besides your critical voice, which blocks you from a particular achievement or particular source of enjoyment, you may find still other blocks to your enjoyment that affect your attitude and receptivity generally. These include:

- Having a high level of stress, so you are nervous about everything generally

- Being out of touch with your feelings, so you tend to be in neutral most of the time

- Being worried about other things, so you keep thinking about them no matter what else you are doing

- A feeling of obligation, which leads you to take on responsibilities and tasks that you don't want to do

You may think of other blocks that affect you. This chapter is designed to help you get rid of these different kinds of blocks.

Overcoming Feelings of Stress

While doing something you enjoy can be a great way to overcome stress, if you are highly stressed about something—or tend to feel a high level of stress generally—your stress can overwhelm your feelings of enjoyment. It's like a balance scale where you have stress on the one side and enjoyment on the other; if the stress is too heavy, it will weigh down that side of the scale, leaving your feelings of enjoyment hanging helplessly in the air.

That's the experience that Carol had. She exuded stress, not only because she had a constantly busy schedule, but also because she didn't like most of the tasks she was doing. But she kept doing what she did and kept accepting more tasks out of sense of obligation and responsibility. Besides being an elementary school teacher and battling her boredom of teaching third-grade students every day, she had numerous faculty and parent-teacher meetings to attend. After school she volunteered in a candy-stripers program at a local hospital, because she didn't want to turn the head of the volunteers down. And she had her own teenage children to deal with, a husband who expected her to prepare dinner each night, plus her mother who lived at home with them and had her own set of demands. Carol was continually feeling drained, as she soldiered on, and when she did try to do something to relax, she was so wound up she couldn't relax, as often replays of the day's stresses intruded.

For Carol and anyone feeling overly stressed, a first step is to seek more balance in life by cutting down on the overload of activities that are causing stress. To this end, you can use some of the techniques discussed in previous chapters for choosing to do less by prioritizing what's important and learning to say no to things you don't want to do, without feeling guilty or apologetic for turning something down. If you really are burdened down by spending too much time doing what you don't want to do, you can't just meditate, visualize, or exercise yourself out of feeling overly stressed so that you experience more enjoyment. Even trying to turn these overwhelming activities into a kind of fun game using some of the approaches described later won't usually work. You just have too much on your plate to enjoy the meal; being overstuffed is causing you pain and you can't sugarcoat the problem with enjoyment. You've got to take care of the pain first, just like in Abraham Maslow's hierarchy of needs; you can't satisfy the higher level needs for belonging, prestige, or self-actualization if you haven't first satisfied the basic needs for survival, safety, and security.

Thus, look at what you can eliminate from your work or your personal life that is causing you pain, so you have more time in your life for activities you enjoy. Just list your various responsibilities, note how much time they are taking each week, and rate them from 1–5 on how much pain and stress they are causing you. Then, multiply the level of stress by the number of hours to come up with your Weekly Stress Score, and think about how you can eliminate the biggest stresses from your life—or at least reduce the time you spend on them, thereby reducing your score. You can use the following chart to help you with the process.

Getting in Touch with Your Feelings

Not being in touch with your feelings can be another block to enjoyment. This can occur if you tend to be emotionally flat, so you are literally going through life in neutral, not experiencing the high or sense of flow that comes from really enjoying and being involved in something. You may avoid feeling the pain, like someone who is constantly feeling stressed, but you don't experience the pleasure either.

A good example of this is Jim, who turned off his feelings when he was a young child, to avoid the pain he experienced being around his parents. They were continually arguing and yelling at each other, and at times his father was variously absent

Major Sources of Stress			
Activities Causing Stress	Hours per Week	Level of Stress (from 1–5)	Weekly Stress Score (Hours × Rating)

or a strong taskmaster when he was home. Meanwhile, his mother was frequently in a bad mood because she felt so much pressure from working too hard both in a very dull clerical job and at home doing household chores. Being a perfectionist, who wanted a sparkling clean house, only added to her feelings of stress. To avoid becoming depressed by all the negativity, Jim pulled back, like a turtle retreating into its shell, and dulled his feelings. As he grew up and had a chance to finally break away from his parents, the emotional shutdown continued. He had developed the habit of shutting down, so he wasn't used to feeling anything.

This kind of emotional deadening is actually harder to deal with than overcoming stress, because the latter involves mainly eliminating the causal factors and feelings of guilt from your life. But here you have to create a new way of feeling that can go beyond opening up. You have to learn to feel feelings you haven't learned to feel before.

So how do you start? One way might be to try to remember back to what you really liked doing as a child before you learned to shut down, so you can recapture this early feeling. Another might be to notice what gives you a more positive feeling than anything else, even if that feeling is only very slight or fleeting, such as watching a movie, eating a dessert you like the taste of, or recalling a time when someone praised you for doing something. Then, take some time to quietly reflect on this childhood or recent feeling and imagine that you are experiencing this event now. Next, project yourself into the scene and notice how you are feeling. Continue the process for a minute or two, both experiencing what is happening and noticing your feelings. Later, when you are doing something that you like doing, recall those feelings, so you can draw on them to enjoy whatever you are doing more.

Another technique might be to do something that causes you to feel physical pleasure, such as getting a massage or swimming, since experiencing any kind of physical enjoyment can help to override the mental and emotional blocks for your feelings, since the limbic system is the most primitive part of your brain. Those sensations are less mediated and controlled by the higher brain centers. Then, pay particular attention to those pleasurable sensations, so you are more aware of them and can call on them, as reminders of how you felt when you enjoyed something, when you are engaged in other activities.

You might also work with a partner or counselor to help you tap into your feelings. For example, as you recall experiences or visualize something positive and inspiring, your partner or counselor might ask you to become aware of your feelings, asking you: "What are you feeling now?" again and again, so that you are forced to pay attention to your body and any sensations you are feeling. The process can increase your awareness, both by having you observe what you are experiencing and articulating it into words.

Stop Thinking of Things That Worry You

As the popular song goes: "Don't worry, be happy." Well, that's exactly what you should do—by shifting your attention away from things that worry you. It's much like what the Buddhists do when they are meditating and intruding thoughts arrive. They acknowledge those thoughts and then turn their focus back onto the word or the stillness of thinking that is at the center of their meditation.

You can use various processes to shift your attention, much as you would to screen out judgmental thoughts and fears.

- Tell the worries to "Go away," and imagine them disappearing or flying away.

- Acknowledge that you do feel a concern, but then force your attention to something else, so after initially acknowledging the concern, you ignore it.

- Use a trigger to remind you to shift your attention to something else each time you experience a worried thought.

- Engage in an activity you really like and throw yourself into it as intensely as possible, so you may even experience the sense of flow that comes with total involvement. Then, any thoughts or worries will automatically disappear because you are so totally involved in the "now."

- Use a physical motion to send any worries away, such as

flicking your wrist or stamping your foot, while you visualize the worries leaving you with each gesture.

- Write down your worries on a sheet of paper and throw that paper into a fire or hold it over a candle until it burns up. Then, as the paper with your worries burns, imagine that your worries are being burned up too, so you feel purified and cleansed of these worries.

- Go through a cognitive reasoning process for each worry, in which you confront that worry with the reasons it doesn't make sense.

- Use your imagination to create a scenario in which your worry leaves and goes away for good. For example, you might see a worry about a person you want out of your life take the form of that person knocking on your door. You open it and tell that person to go away. Then you see the person suddenly being blown down a path by a strong gust of wind, disappearing into the sunset and falling with a big splash into the water, never to return.

Use whichever approach or combination of approaches works best for you; and sometimes use different approaches for different types of worries. For example, you might confront an unreasonable worry with reason; you might imagine a real worry disappearing as you burn it up; you might greet another worry with a brief acknowledgment and then turn away. Or combine a selection of these techniques, especially if you find a specific worry especially persistent so it keeps coming back. Try different approaches to emphasize that it isn't welcome, and with repetition, that worry will finally go away.

Overcoming Feelings of Obligation

A sense of obligation that goes too far can turn into a joy killer, too, particularly when you feel obligated to take on so many responsibilities that you become stressed out from overwork. A simple response, already suggested in the discussion of getting rid of stress, is to say no to something new when you are already doing too much. Or put that new responsibility on a shelf until you have more free time and can deal with it then.

Another approach is to look at all of your promises and commitments to carry out certain obligations, and assess the relative importance or "must do" nature of each one, along with the time you have to spend on that obligation, much like in the process of evaluating stressors. Then, examine which obligations are the least necessary and/or are taking the most time, so you can drop those obligations. To do so, multiply the hours you spend on an unwanted obligation each week by the degree to which you feel it is unnecessary. Then, as practical, drop the obligations that are taking the most time and are least desirable to you.

After you go through the process and decide what obligations to drop, this choice may require some explaining to someone why you can't take on or carry out a particular task after the fact. But be ready to stand your ground firmly, so you don't end up getting talked into taking on that obligation again.

You can use the chart on the following page to help you review and eliminate your unwanted obligations.

Another approach to getting rid of unwanted obligations is to do a visualization in which you see yourself getting rid of that obligation. To do this, take some time to get relaxed in a quiet place. Then, ask yourself what obligations you feel are unnecessary or unwanted. Pick the first one or the one you feel most strongly you want to get rid of. See yourself stop doing that task or activity. If you have to tell someone you are no longer going to do that task, do so, and see yourself firmly saying no, you aren't going to do it anymore. Finally, see yourself turning away from doing that obligation and walking away. As you do, you

Major Obligations to Do or Say No To			
Major Obligations to Consider Dropping	Hours per Week	How Unnecessary (from 0–5)	Weekly Drop-It Score (Hours × Rating)

feel very good and satisfied that you don't have to do that unwanted task anymore.

If other obligations start to block your enjoyment, become aware of what they are and then think of ways to eliminate them. You can adapt any of the techniques described here, such as saying no to that block, visualizing it gone, or otherwise reducing it or getting out of your life.

PART III

101 Ways to Enjoy
Yourself More at Work

8

Add More Fun to the Workplace

You can add fun to whatever kind of work you are doing, whether you want to be doing it or not. Some techniques include turning routine work into a kind of personal game or contest, spicing up your workplace environment, or creating fun things to do on your breaks. This chapter will focus on things you can do yourself—though you might involve others, too; the next chapters focus on things to do with others you work with.

1. Make Routine Work More Interesting

There's no getting around it. Certain types of work can become very tedious, such as entering names and numbers into a database, typing up lists of people, sorting papers and organizing files, copying documents, and the like. They are necessary but involve routine and often tedious tasks.

You can perk up the routine in various ways:

- Create a race for yourself—or with others who are doing similar work. Imagine you are trying to be the first to process a certain number of documents or complete a file or page of information—or see how many documents, files, or pages you can complete in a certain amount of time. You may even want to set an alarm or timer to start the clock ticking, and either try to beat your own record or race one or more other employees to see who can do it fastest. Then, have a prize for the winner—or give yourself a reward if you surpass a previous record. The advantage of this game is it helps to make you more productive as you try to win.

• Give yourself a quick reward at the end of completing a task or at the end of a certain amount of time doing routine work. For example, reward yourself with a tasty snack after you have been doing something tedious for an hour or give yourself reward points that you can accumulate to get a desired reward after your work is over for the day. You'll not only enjoy the reward, but just thinking about enjoying the reward, as you do something routine, particularly if it's boring, can provide you with some stimulating anticipation that helps to make the time fly. (This is also a great technique to use on a long drive, or if you have a long commute, as I found on my six-hour commutes to a satellite office I set up in L.A. I used assorted mind exercises that helped me stay alert and energized because they gave me something interesting to imagine or think about as I drove—though if you find this visualization or thinking distracts you, don't do these while you drive. I also planned on little rewards for myself, like a quick stop for a snack or making cell phone calls along the way for about ten minutes every hour and a half or so.)

• Listen to some music, and if you are in an office with others and this isn't a collective choice to listen, you can use ear phones, so no one else has to hear what you are listening to. If necessary, get approval to do this from higher-ups in the office. Point out how this will make you more aware and efficient and won't distract you from what you are doing. Or offer to demonstrate that this works if you get any resistance to this fun idea.

2. Dress Up Your Desk, Workspace, or Office

The idea here is to create a more inviting office environment for yourself, for meeting with customers or clients, or for your workplace generally. In doing so, get some fun knickknacks to liven up the space—and you can use this to express your personality, too. For example, one banker who got the nickname "The Purple Lady" had all manner of purple objects on her desk, in addition to often coming to work wearing purple adornments or clothing. Many of her customers brought in small purple items to add to her collection. For example, she had small purple cars, some purple flowers, a purple notebook, a collection of purple pens and pencils, a CD with a mostly purple cover, and so on. Besides being a statement of "this is me," the purple knickknacks also provided a great conversational opener that helped to set her clients at ease, and besides being fun, they contributed to her good personal rapport with clients, which made her one of the highest earning bankers at that firm.

3. Nibble While You Work

As long as you can do so comfortably and without interfering with your work, have something to nibble or drink beside you, so you can take an occasional bite or sip of something to break up your work. You can easily use low-calorie and healthy snacks when you do this, such as fruit juice, no-calorie sodas, carrot sticks, and the like if you are diet-conscious or watching your weight. And consider making these creative taste-treat adventures, where you try out new snacks and drinks, while keeping your overall diet and daily calorie count in mind. You'll find your local supermarket, deli, convenience store, or gourmet boutique filled with these—from exotic nuts, chopped fruit bits, and trail mixes to combos covered with yogurt and chocolate. And today there are all sorts of combinations of juices and protein drinks you can try. Even miniboxes or minibags of cereals might be ideal for these workday taste treats.

4. Take a Stretch or Exercise Break

Another way to invigorate your work—literally—is to take a quick stretch or exercise break every hour or so for a couple of minutes. You can do this sitting down or standing up, whatever is more comfortable for you—and what's appropriate for your workplace. Either way, you'll get a recharge of energy as you move about. You might combine this exercise with some affirmations to give you even more positive energy, such as saying something like "I feel great!" or "I'm full of enthusiasm and energy," as you swing your body from left to right, stretch yourself as tall as you can, stamp your foot, or raise and lower your hand in a fist, and feel the energy course through you.

5. Visualize Yourself Having Fun

If you are doing routine work that doesn't involve much concentration, you might try imagining yourself engaging in some fun activity. Keep your eyes open as you do this. The process is a little like letting your imagination go while you are in a relaxed meditative state, except that you are fully conscious and placing most of your attention on what you are doing, so you continue doing it effectively (which naturally has to come first, since you're at work). But you can break up the boredom of doing something that's dull by employing the "split mind" technique, so while you are consciously doing your job, you are also visualizing yourself having a fun experience doing something else. What else? It can be whatever you want—taking a vacation trip to the wilderness, imagining yourself soaring in a plane, going on a cruise through the tropics, meeting the man or woman of your dreams, anything. But keep it light, so the part of your mind that is working is always ready to step in to pull you back if you start to get too involved in your visualization. This way you do some fun mind traveling while you work, but you don't go too far away, so you can't quickly come right back.

6. Listen to Songs in Your Head

If you can't listen to music through your headphones, you might be able to trigger your own play list in your head. If you really enjoy music, and you have learned the melodies and/or the lyrics, you might be able to hear them just by calling them forth while you work. If so, just let the music or lyrics flow through you; don't struggle to remember. This way you can enjoy the music without interfering with your work; you just tune your attention, like switching a knob on the radio, to listen to the song. For example, even though he was deaf, Beethoven was able to hear and compose a song in his mind. If you're into writing music, you might even be able to create some original songs this way. Otherwise, just listen to something you already know. However, if the music doesn't quickly come to you, don't use this technique—it'll be too distracting from doing your work.

7. Replay TV Shows or Movies in Your Mind

Still another way to enliven a routine job is to recall a recent TV show or movie you have seen and imagine that you are seeing it now on your mental screen. While this experience can be even more intense when you get relaxed and close your eyes, don't try this while you are at work. Instead, just use your split mind to visualize the scene from the TV show or movie playing out in front of you, while you are doing something else. For example, as I'm typing this, I'm seeing a car chase from a film I saw a few nights ago racing in front of my mind. And then there's a guy from the *Picking Daisies* show bending down and bringing a guy back from the dead with a touch to ask him some questions about his murder, before he sends him back again.

This technique is ideal to use if you are good at visualizing; or if you are not initially, you might develop this ability by practicing at home in a quiet place where you can close your eyes and see the scenes play out in front of you on the mental screen in your mind's eye. Then, once you see a scene vividly play out for you, try opening your eyes while you continue to concentrate on that experience. Gradually, you will become increasingly able to see the scene with your eyes open. Once you are, try doing this in an everyday environment, such as when you are taking a walk in the park, sitting on a bench waiting for a bus, or doing errands (but not while you're driving). Then, once you feel comfortable doing this in a non-work setting, try doing it at work. Start the process by evoking these images while you are on a break, doing nothing else, so you can better concentrate on calling forth these images. Then, once you are able to do that, try calling up a scene while you are doing some routine work where you don't have to pay close attention. Soon this process may become second nature to you—it's like being at the movies at work.

8. Have a Conversation with Yourself

A close cousin to these visualization and listening techniques is to have a discussion, debate, or other type of conversation with yourself as you work at something you don't have to think too much about doing. Pick some topic, any topic, and then experience different parts of yourself engaged in this interchange. You might even give these different parts of yourself different names, from those you make up to people you know. Then, without doing much to direct it, let the conversation go back and forth in your mind.

You can also use the self-talk technique to help clarify your thoughts about a particular concern you have or about a current issue in the news. Start the process by making a statement about the issue or asking a question, such as "What should I do about . . . ?" or "What do I think about . . . ?" And then let the conversation begin, as different parts of yourself state different ideas or opinions. This is also a useful technique you can take home with you, and for more depth, get relaxed in a quiet place and close your eyes. But at work you can start the conversation, and use the part of yourself that is alert and attentive to your work to keep you from getting too engrossed with your conversation so you get distracted from your work. After all, the goal is to have fun working while staying engaged and productive—not to let the internal dialogue take you away from your work.

9. Dress Up Your Day

One way to stir up the office is to get dressed up, as if for a special occasion. This is something you might do from time to time so you look and feel special. It's an especially good approach when there's something you're celebrating. And if you can get others to dress up, too, such as by selecting a particular day with others at work, you can turn this into a workplace event. Whether you do this yourself or as a group, you can show off your finery during breaks, at lunch, or after work. You might even turn this into a mini-fashion show.

If you are into one of the part-time fashion sales programs, this could even be a way to show off the types of clothing you represent. Be careful you don't tread on any company policies about personal selling—but if your company's fine with this, you're not only finding a way to enjoy your work more, but make some additional income, too.

10. Whistle and Sing While You Work

Still another way to liven up things at work, if you've got the voice for this, is to regale the people at work with a song or musical interlude. Or perhaps invite others to join in to create a small chorus. Play it by ear to make sure this approach will be acceptable—and perhaps prepare the way by mentioning your idea to a few of your work pals. Then, if they're receptive, at least you know you'll have a small appreciative audience to set the tone with others.

Pick a lively, upbeat song, and then at an opportune moment, serenade the office, and if there's a familiar chorus, encourage others to join in. You might even bring a guitar, harmonica, or other easy-to-carry instrument to accompany yourself. You'll find this is a great way to lift everyone's spirit in many offices—though if you find your office mates are uptight about someone bursting into song, you can always do your singing in your imagination to yourself or wait till everyone clears out for lunch and treat yourself to a short medley.

11. Bring Your Pet to Work

In some offices, pets—assuming they are well-disciplined and quiet—are welcome. If your company allows this, you might bring your dog, cat, or other creature to work with you. Just like many dogs and even cats have proved to be great visitors and companions in cheering up hospital patients or residents of a senior citizen home, so they can bring lightness and love to your office. Be sure you have a well-behaved, sociable (and toilet-trained) pet who will welcome the attention—and you should stay around as others in the office enjoy petting and playing with your pet.

You can make the event even more special if you dress up your pet (maybe you can dress up, too). Today, there are all kinds of fun costumes, mostly for dogs, available through pet boutiques or online sales. You might also bring along some small quiet toys for your pet to play with, so he or she doesn't get bored when you are through showing off and it's time to go back to work.

Still another possibility is bringing in a fish tank with gold-fish or exotic fish. They can be very relaxing and intriguing to watch, especially if you are seeking a minibreak where instead of meditating or visualizing for a minute or two, you watch your fish. You may find that others in the office enjoy coming to watch your fish as well.

12. Find a Fun Mascot to Adorn Your Workspace

Remember the Purple Lady who adorned her desk and sur-roundings with purple objects? Well, an alternative to collecting a lot of objects is to pick out a mascot and make that the focus of your display. And then you might use that mascot to cheer up others in the office by leaving it around the workplace.

For example, one insurance executive adopted a rubber toy gorilla as a mascot and from time to time left him in unusual places around the office, especially when others were having a hard day, to cheer everyone up.[1] To find a mascot, you might go to your local toy store or gift shop and find a creature that would be a suitable addition for you and your office. Some great possi-bilities are giraffes, monkeys, lions, tigers, dogs, cats, whatever catches your fancy. You may choose a big rubber animal or you may go for something furry and cuddly. Or you may want to go for something unusual that will evoke comments and amusement, like a big furry snake or iguana. The idea is to pick out something that seems upbeat and cheery and evokes smiles, good feelings, and interaction with others.

13. Have a Ball at Work

Another way to liven up the work day is with a ball—though make it something light and soft, so you don't do any damage when you play with it. For example, bring in a Nerf ball, a soft-foam ball that comes in various shapes and sizes (such as a basketball or football shape). Then, for a relaxation break, you can toss it up and down at your desk, or perhaps toss it to another willing co-worker or start a Nerf toss volley, where others in the office join in, too. Of course, make sure that you have management that is receptive to your having a ball for a brief break at work.

Another possibility, if you have a long hallway in your office, is to set up some empty boxes and roll a soft Nerf ball or beach ball down the hall, so you play a quick frame or two of office bowling. You might even create some bowling teams to compete after hours or during lunch breaks at who hits the most boxes when you roll your balls.

Or you can put up a hoop on your office door so you can throw a Nerf or Koosh basketball when you take a break—and invite others to join you for a few quick tosses before you go back to work.

14. Open an Art Gallery in Your Office

If you have an enclosed office—or can requisition a wall for this, create an art gallery where you show off some art pieces you really like—and change what you are showing from time to time. Aside from bringing in art from your home, you can invite others in the office to contribute their own art pieces, or even have a special "opening" when the new pictures go up and turn this into a party or open-house drop-in during certain hours.

15. Show Off Your Collection

Is there anything you are especially fond of? Do you already have a collection at home? In either case, you can start a collection of certain types of objects for the office, or bring a sampling of items from your home collection. It's a great conversation starter for others in the office, and ideal for breaking the ice if you are dealing with new customers. Collections can be of almost anything—owls, penguins, postcards, you name it. And some collections lend themselves to an interactive component, such as one woman who collected all kinds of hats and brought them to work, where she posted them on a wall near the coffee maker and invited people to try wearing one of her hats for a day. As described by Dave Hemsath and Leslie Yerkes in their book *301 Ways to Have Fun at Work*, the hats were a big hit and started a lot of lively conversations.[2]

16. Gather Fun Ideas in a Fun Box

While this can be done individually, say by setting aside a file or drawer in your desk to collect these bits of fun trivia, this can be turned into a basis for a group sharing, or everyone can exchange or pass on their files to others. Then, as the file or material in the box grows too big, create another file or box for fun items—and later you can always go back and review the archives.

17. Collect Cartoons or Jokes

Try starting a daily cartoon or joke sharing. Just bring in a few cartoons or jokes to start off the process and invite others to bring in their favorite cartoons or jokes that they've encountered in the daily newspaper, discovered online, or received in an email. Then, before work, during breaks, or at lunch, pass them around.

Or try coming up with your own humorous captions for photos from newspapers or magazines and invite others to add their own ideas. To do so, put up a picture on the door of your office or a centrally located place, near the water cooler, for example, or in the break room, and provide a pen, pencil, or crayons nearby so people can easily add their comments.

18. Post Puzzles, Paper Games, or Riddles

Another way to add lightness and humor to the workplace is to post puzzles, games from the local newspaper, or riddles for others to peruse when they are waiting to do something else, like make some copies at the copy machine, or when on a break. One good source of these puzzles and games is the local newspaper, especially the one from Sunday. If you bring in crossword puzzles, invite people to see how many words they can solve in the puzzle in a short time (say five minutes) and add those words. Or look for short easy-to-solve puzzles or quick-to-play games. For instance, you might use some of the fill-in-the-blanks puzzles, a Sudoku teaser, or a frame game, where you have to figure out what common expression or phrase is spelled out by several symbols and cartoon images. Other possibilities include small wooden and plastic puzzles, like a Rubik's Cube. You could also turn these puzzles and games into a fun competition, where you offer a small prize, ribbon, free lunch, or the like, to the winner.

19. Share Funny Letters and E-Mails

Have you gotten any funny letters or e-mails in the course of doing your job? It's fun to share them with others and invite others to share their own funny letters or e-mails—as long as you do this on breaks or your company feels comfortable with you taking a minute or two to perk up your work day in this. You also want to be sure any e-mails are in the spirit of good fun, not mean-spirited or used to embarrass a colleague or client. Some examples of these light-hearted letters and e-mails might be dumb questions and comments, like: "What time is the 9 o'clock meeting?" Or parents might bring in something funny written by their kids, like the comments I collected in *When I Grow up I Want to Be a Sturgeon: And Other Wrong Things Kids Write* (Seattle, Wash.: Sasquatch Books, 2006). Here are a few of my favorites: "He was known as a cereal killer," "A rolling stone gathers no mess," and "A cliché is a common expression that has become old hat." Depending on what works best in your workplace, you might send these out as e-mails to selected individual members of your department or to everyone—or simply bring in print-outs with you and pass them around.

20. Collect or Create a Top Ten List

You can start by collecting a Top Ten list, such as the Top Ten list on the Dave Letterman show, which is commonly available online. Then, circulate it to others in an e-mail or post it by the water cooler, coffee pot, or in the lunch area.

Then, take the Top Ten list to the next level by inviting people to create their own or contribute to one that is circulated around the office. Invite people to come up with Top Ten lists that feature current events, pop culture, or things about the office. For example, some possibilities might be: "The Top Ten reasons that Barry Bonds isn't going to play baseball with the Giants," "The

Top Ten ways that the new mayor/president might celebrate his/ her victory," "The Top Ten reasons why we are going to beat our biggest competitor in sales next month." Once you've chosen a topic, come up with ten ideas yourself or circulate the list and invite others to contribute to it—the first ten make the list. Or you can all vote on the best ideas and that becomes the official Top Ten list for that day.

21. Send Out a Joke E-Mail to Others in the Office

As long as this isn't against your office policy (do check with HR first), you might start the day or send out an e-mail at lunchtime with a favorite joke or the joke-of-the-day—and you might invite others to add their own joke and pass on the e-mail. And later, you might even compile these into a booklet of everyone's favorite jokes that you can print up and give to everyone or post on a bulletin board for everyone to see.

Such jokes might be short one-liners, funny sayings, humorous Top Ten lists—just keep them brief. And if you are creative, try coming up with your own funny sayings and jokes.

22. Create a Humorous Voice Mail

This may not work well if you're in a company that wants to keep customer contact serious, such as if you work in a bank or a funeral parlor. However, in other settings, you can spice up your phone messages with a comment that gives callers a laugh—and these messages are fun to think up, too. For example, one history instructor taped his messages to students as if he was a historical character. As Abe Lincoln, he told one student: "Four score and seven years ago, your paper was due."[3]

Similarly, you might leave messages as any character you want to be, drawing on literature, politics, films, or TV. Or program your voice mail, so when someone calls, they get a message from a character, such as a cowboy from the Old West announcing in a Western twang: "Howdy, pardner. You've missed the round-up, but if you want to leave a message, we'll get back to you lickety-split." Or choose a sophisticated fashion persona, a hard-driving real estate mogul, you name it. Just think of the Geico company, which used a caveman to get out their insurance message—and their cavemen characters even made it onto a TV show. So it may seem a little corny, but it's fun.

23. Show Off Your Cooking or Catering Skills

If you enjoy cooking or creating fancy hors d'oeuvres for parties, bring in one of your creations to give everyone a taste treat during a break or lunchtime. For this, easy-to-share items are good, such as homebaked cookies and cut-up veggie wraps.

24. Draw and Craft Your Way to Fun

Whether you think of yourself as an artist or not, you can take a few minutes during a break or while your computer is starting up to create some fun artsy-craftsy pieces just for you or to share with others in the office. In *How to Draw a Radish and Other Fun Things to Do at Work*, Joy Sikorski provides an amusing arsenal of ways to perk up your work and workplace with arts and crafts.[4] In addition to the usual supplies found in most offices (paper, pencil, pen, paperclips), other items on your to-get list might include rub-on dots, scissors, glue stick, tape, chalk, rubber stamps, and paper bags.[5] Some of the things to do on your break might be:

•   With a pen or pencil draw some quick cartoon sketches, such as of a wren, kitty cat, chick, sleeping dog, or a dog and bird fight.[6] Other possibilities she suggests with quickie illustrations include water, an island, a palm tree, the sun, sunglasses, mountains, molehills, a gift, a mouse, a suitcase, birds, a tadpole, a worm, a school of fish, a boat, a sinking boat, and fancy alphabets.[7]

- Create a mobile by cutting out and taping pictures of things you like to both sides of $1\frac{1}{2}''$ or $2''$ squares. Then, laminate both sides with transparent tape and hand them with different lengths of tread from a lamp or your ceiling—or you can punch holes in the squares to make a necklace that you intersperse with paperclips.[8]

- Create a jigsaw puzzle by cutting up a postcard. Put the pieces in an envelope and pull them out to reassemble the puzzle later. Of course, the larger the pieces, the easier it will be to do.[9]

- Collect pictures of your co-workers as babies and create a collage.[10] You might post these at your workspace, in the lunch room, or on an office bulletin board. You might also have a contest to see who can identify the most.

- Turn a ruler or stick into a magic wand and offer to grant wishes or change someone into something—in their imagination, of course.[11]

- Turn your lunch bag into a variety of fun objects—such as a kite, hat, puppet, mask, serving dish, or bracelet—with the snip of some scissors and some tape or string.[12]

- Shred or tear up some paper or a collage you have created to make confetti. Sikorski suggests small squares, but you can cut or tear these small pieces any way you want.[13] Then, at an opportune time, such as during a break for lunch, throw them up in the air and call out "Yea!" Or invite others in the office to do the same so you do this together, like you're giving a group cheer. This can be especially good to create or keep for special occasions, such as celebrating a big sale or someone's birthday or promotion.

- Write on a banana with a ballpoint pen.[14] Or try writing on other easy-to-write-on fruit, such as an apple or pear. Try writing a funny saying, or an affirmation such as "I feel great!" Then, you might present this to someone else as a novelty gift from you.

- Create some origami by folding a piece of paper into different shapes, such as paper boats and balloons.[15] You can also use this technique to amaze others as you show them how to quickly turn an ordinary sheet of paper into something wonderful.

- Create a little booklet with illustrations, poems, quotes, sayings, or whatever you want by folding a sheet of paper twice (once in half the long way, then in half again) to create a $4^{1}/_{4}'' \times 5^{1}/_{2}''$ booklet.[16] Then, draw on each section, and afterwards you can make copies to share with others in the office.

25. Place Humorous Reminders Around the Office

You can use Post-its, bumper stickers, or stickers to remind yourself and others to engage in certain behaviors. For instance, to remind people to smile, put up smiley faces or signs with the word "Smile" on them or put them on Post-its by the phones of people in sales and customer service. To encourage people to use humor, scatter Post-its around that say "Laugh" or "Tell a Joke."

26. Create a Good Feelings Chart

If you want to let others know how you feel and whether to approach you or not or how, you might use a wheel with colors or funny characters on it, an idea used by a director of programs for one company in the Midwest.[17] The employees each had a color wheel at their desk like a board game spinner and they each pasted funny pictures in each section to let each other know how they were feeling that day—red for "off limits," yellow for "proceed with caution," green for "come on in."

Similarly, you can create your own mood chart—whether you use a ring of colors, thermometer, barometer, pyramid, or other kind of design. The key is to divide the chart into three to six sections indicating how you are feeling and whether people should approach you. For example, you might create a simple chart divided into sections with these colors and comments to let people know what to do. Put the cartoon picture representing you in the colored section to let you know how you feel. Your chart could be something like this:

Yellow: Feel great—come on in!

Orange: Really busy—approach cautiously!

Red: Feeling frazzled—stay away!

Purple: Feeling tired—come charge me up!

Blue: Feeling blue—cheer me up!

Green: Feeling lucky—got any good ideas?

27. Create an Idea List or Idea Journal

What else would you like to do to have fun at work? Create your own idea list or journal and write down your ideas for fun things to do as you think of them. If others are doing the same, you can share your lists with one another—and later, you can start to implement some of your ideas. I guarantee as you think about more fun things to do, you'll increase your enjoyment and have more fun at work.

9

Make Work More Fun for Everyone

Besides adding fun to the workplace on your own—or mostly on your own—there are ways to make having fun a group activity for your department or division or for the whole office. You can do this as either an employee taking a leadership role or if you are a manager or company owner adding fun activities to increase moral and productivity. The focus here is on fun activities that you can introduce to others you work with in your own office—though potentially, these ideas can spread throughout a larger company, too.

28. Create a Fun List or Fun Box for Your Office

What would other people in your office like to do to make the workplace more fun—and increase morale, performance, and productivity, too? Find out by inviting people to add their suggestions to a fun list that you circulate via hard copy or e-mail. Start it off with a brief explanation and a few suggestions of your own to get everyone started, and then let the ideas pour in. Or you can use a Fun Box—essentially a suggestion box for fun ideas—which people can add to anonymously or using their name. Invite people to volunteer to organize any activities that involve the group, such as a picnic or party. You can mention any of the ideas you especially like from this book or come up with your own. And offer rewards for the best suggestions, with contributions provided by each employee kicking in a little (say $1–5).

29. Turn on Some Music to Make Routine Work Go Faster

If people are doing fairly routine, repetitive work that doesn't require much concentration, suggest that you might have some music in the background—provided everyone can agree on what type of music to play. If not, people can always bringing in their own iPods or other players and headphones to listen individually. But it can create a nice community spirit if you all listen together. And customers might enjoy the music too and buy more as a result. For example, my local Safeway often has music playing over the PA system, which the clerks really enjoy—typically light rock or contemporary country. I often find myself singing along to a song I like and I see other shoppers doing the same.

To add music, you might start by inviting people to give their opinions at a meeting or on an e-mail you circulate. Ask whether they would like to hear music while they work and then ask what kind. Ask people if they have their own CDs or MP3s they might like to bring in. In fact, as long as everyone's game for it, this might be a way to feature different music styles. For example, if people come from diverse backgrounds, you can introduce music from different cultures—which is a great way to create multicultural awareness and understanding.

30. Encourage Others to Decorate Their Desks or Workspaces

Besides festooning your own desk, cubicle, or office with art-work, photos, or fun toys, you might encourage others to do so, and then when people acquire new objects, they can show them off to others, which is both fun and contributes to bonding with others at the office. It can also give you some insights into who people are—their interests, hobbies, family members, favorite colors, and the like, which can help everyone better relate to their fellow staff members. For anyone who has watched *Big Brother*, the summer TV show where cameras follow a group of people around 24–7, there's this kind of moment when the new Head of Household shows off his or her Head of Household bed-room. The HOH invites everyone to come look at the new "HOH room," and then everyone (or almost everyone) follows him or her into the room, and they walk around expressing their "ohhs" and "ahhs," along with their occasional comments, re-actions, and insights to learning about their housemate and his or her family in a new way.

31. Have a Party Where People Decorate Their Workspace

Consider this a fun way for people to relax during a lunch break or after work. Provide some basic art supplies (such as paper, colored markers, crayons, tape, old magazines, glue sticks, etc.) or invite people to bring their own. Then, everyone spends a half-hour or hour creating some designs or collages, which can be displayed in designated places, such as around the coffee pot, in the halls, in people's offices or cubicles, or on people's desks. Clients might find this enjoyable to look at, too, and the art can be a great conversation starter. Later, you can always have another party and put up the new art.

32. Organize Special Dress-Up Days

Some companies already have a casual-dress day on Fridays or ask employees to come in costume for holidays like Halloween and Christmas. But if your company doesn't, you and some other employees might try to organize this yourself—with the blessings of the company owner or top managers, of course. While casual-dress days are common (where it isn't already the way people dress every day), try going the other way to have a special dress-up day from time to time. Then, everyone comes dressed in their finest, from tuxes for the men to gowns for the women. And to add to the occasion, invite everyone to bring some gourmet specialties to enjoy during lunch or after work.

33. Create a Bingo Awards Game for the Work You Do

This isn't just playing bingo—it's doing your work and achieving whatever you can as quickly as possible to score. The way to do this is to create a list of activities you want to reward, such as getting a customer to order a particular product or service, completing a certain number of letters, writing up some promotional materials, making a certain number of phone calls to clients, etc. You and other employees can develop the list. Then, scatter these items on a series of Work Bingo cards, using the usual 5 × 5 matrix, or to make it smaller and easier to complete, use a 4 × 4 or even a 3 × 3 matrix. Give each employee a Work Bingo card, and then, as each employee completes a task on his or her card, he or she crosses it off with a magic marker. If you want to encourage employees to work together, allow them to trade cards, exchange tasks, or do a task for another employee. Whoever is in charge of that task gets the credit. Then, when an employee gets five in a row (or four or three with a 4 × 4 or 3 × 3 matrix, respectively), he or she yells out "Bingo!" and gets a prize, which might be contributed by the employer or by employees pooling small contributions together (say $1 to $5 each) to buy these inexpensive prizes.

I observed one such Bingo game in a business referral network I belong to. The idea was to bring in more guests to meetings as well as make referrals to other people in the group. So the game organizers used relevant categories, such as bringing a guest, having a guest become a new member, giving a business referral to another member, having another member get some work as a result of a business referral, and so on. The event was very successful, and at the end, the members who got Bingos received prizes in the form of donated products and services from other members of the group.

34. Take a Goofy Break to Unwind

This is a good way to relieve tension if you work in a high-stress workplace or have just completed a big deadline. While you can take your own personal goofy break, say by putting on a funny hat or drawing some funny cartoons, it's even more fun if you can involve your office mates, too, so you participate in some goofy activities together. Like showing off objects on a desk or wall, this is a great way to bond with others in the office.

In some cases, you need to prepare by getting the materials for goofing off together, such as if you want to stage a marshmallow fight or have a Nerf gun battle, with employees organized into teams. But otherwise, you can use objects already in the office, such as staging a relay race with the office chairs (preferably using chairs with wheels), or spinning your office chairs around for a quick break in the routine.[1] But whatever you do, keep these activities to break times, before the work day begins, or after work ends—and make sure top managers agree. In some companies, managers promote such activities as a way of enthusing the troops and furthering team building.

35. Create a Humorous Penalty Jar

Having a penalty jar where people have to put a small amount of money every time they break one of the office "rules" is a great way to discourage unwanted behavior as well as have fun. Of course, this should be restricted to less serious forms of behavioral gaffes, which can be handled with a lighthearted touch. For anything serious, the problem must be dealt with seriously, probably involving the company owner, boss, or top management. But for other kinds of minor faux pas, take it away.

For example, some behaviors that might merit a fun penalty could be uttering a curse word (invite people to choose what words should be included, and put those on a list) that someone else hears, missing a meeting, forgetting an appointment, not making a deadline, etc. Keep the penalties low—say 25 or 50 cents. Then, if there are any financial proceeds after a week or two, use them to provide supplies at office parties or for snacks, like muffins and donuts in the morning or before a meeting. I heard of one company where the employees saved all of the penalty-jar money until the end of the year—when they were able to fully fund a holiday party.

36. Create a Joke-of-the-Day List

Invite people to contribute to a Joke-of-the-Day list by bringing in short jokes, which they post on a bulletin board near the coffee pot or lunch room or send around via e-mail to others in the office. Then, others can contribute short jokes to the bulletin board or add to the e-mail and forward it on.

37. Organize a Fun Committee

Another approach used in some offices is to have a special-activities, events, or fun committee with a few participants devoted to putting together fun recreational activities for the group. The group can invite suggestions from others in the workplace, but then it takes the lead in organizing the activities, which can range from parties and picnics to competitions and contests, with fun awards, which can sometimes be for a good performance or achievement. The business networking group I belong to has a committee that plans special events, from potluck get-togethers to fun contests, such as the Referral Bingo described earlier. Another example, described by Hemsath and Yerkes, are the "Scream Teams" established at a Capital One Services office in Tampa, Florida. The teams are responsible for organizing events, such as theme days when everyone dresses up and brings a potluck dish, and putting on events, like birthday and anniversary celebrations, ceremonies to recognize peers, and community-involvement activities.[2]

38. Organize a Brainstorming Session for Fun Ideas

In addition to having an organized Fun Committee as suggested above, you might organize an occasional brainstorming group to come up with fun ideas. Choose someone to keep a list of ideas and then start generating ideas. You can do this as a group, where people shout out ideas, coming up with as many ideas as come to mind, without trying to censor or critique any ideas. Or if some people are more comfortable brainstorming quietly on their own, ask everyone to pull out a sheet of paper and write down their ideas as they come up with them. Then, after people are finished coming up with ideas, ask people to read their ideas aloud, either one person at a time, or having each person in turn share an idea not already suggested, to be added to the list. After you have collected all the ideas, then vote on which ideas people would like to put into practice. If there are a lot of ideas, ask people to vote "5" for their favorite idea, "4" for the next favorite, and so on for their top five ideas. Then, add up the scores for any items selected and the higher the score, the more popular the item. Afterwards, you can pick one or more ideas to put into practice in your workplace.

39. Develop a Newsletter or Column Featuring Fun Ideas

If your company has a newsletter, you can contribute a column featuring fun ideas. Invite other employees to contribute so this becomes a group effort. Some possible article ideas are: reviews of movies or DVDs, local restaurant reviews, short bits of news about the accomplishments and personal lives of employees, a favorite-jokes column, happenings in the local community, you name it. Or if you don't already have a company newsletter, consider starting one yourself if you think you would enjoy writing and organizing one, with management approval. You'll find having a newsletter contributes to employee bonding and morale. It helps employees better know each other and feel recognized by others for their accomplishments both at work and in their personal life. In addition, the news tidbits can be a great conversation starter. And sometimes you can share the newsletters with customers, too, turning the newsletter into a form of public relations to promote better customer relations.

40. Set Up a Game Shelf for Your Lunch or Break Room

Bring in some of your favorite games and invite other employees to do the same. Then, you can play these games during lunch breaks or after work. Sometimes games can be a good icebreaker for a meeting or training session. They help people feel engaged and get the creative juices flowing.

41. Fun Gag Gifts and Toys Spark Up the Office

Here are some items you might add to your shopping list if you are considering getting a party favor or humorous reward for someone. Or simply add them to a community office toy box, where people can easily play with them during breaks and downtime.

- Nerf balls, swords, guns, and other objects—nice, soft, and fluffy, so they make great things to throw around in the office.

- A Slinky or set of small Slinkys, for draping over chairs or having a fun race down the stairs.

- A Koosh ball or soft stress ball, which you can easily throw or squish when you're feeling stressed or want to be playful.

- Some yo-yos.

- A boss or employee doll, where you can move the arms and legs or push a button to get the doll to say something. (For example, I picked up a plastic boss doll with a big lumpy face at a rummage sale with a button you push, and then he spouts off one of a number of phrases, such as "You're fired" or "Why did you think that stupid idea would work?"

- Silly Putty, to squeeze, shape, and stick to things in the office.

What else can you come up with? Besides visiting your local toy store, a good place to find such objects is in the toy section of your local Salvation Army or Goodwill store, in the toy section of K-Mart or Wal-Mart, online at one of the many virtual stores specializing in novelty products for the workplace (such as happyworker.com, where I got a collection of small boss and money-man dolls).

42. Keep a Humor Manual

Another fun project can be creating a humor manual, in which you collect jokes, cartoons, funny stories, and ideas for having fun. Invite others to contribute to the project; then make copies and put each one in a binder, plastic folder, or spiral-bound booklet. These humor booklets can make great gifts for holiday parties, award ceremonies, or other occasions. The ideas in these books can also be used as a kickoff for a meeting or training session or to spice up a lunch or after-work get-together with others from the office.

43. Play a Change-the-Names-and-Titles Game

To spice up office communications, invite people to pick new names and titles to identify themselves and what they do. And if people like the change enough, they might even keep their new names and titles—at least for others in the workplace, though they still should use their regular names and titles for interactions with customers, who aren't in on the joke.

For example, employees might adopt exotic or foreign names, like Natasha or Sir Wellington, famous names in history, like Churchill or Attila the Hun, or animal identities, such as Tiger or Mustang. Titles might become something imaginative, such as Queen of Literary Pleasures for a senior editor; Goddess of Delights for an arts coordinator; and Chancellor of the Exchequer for a financial planner. Then, employees might use these names and titles with each other and even put them on their doors, voice mail, or handmade stationery.

44. Put Up a Goal-and-Achievements Chart

While this is typically something management does, if there isn't one, employees can create it themselves. Create a weekly or monthly chart on a large poster board, which you can display on the wall for all to see. Place the goal to be achieved at the top right and the starting point (whether where you are today or at a beginning point in the recent past) in the lower left. Then, start a line toward the goal, and use a colored dot or cartoon image of a person or animal to show how the group or department is progressing toward that goal.

For example, the goal might be achieving a certain level of sales, attracting a certain number of clients, closing a certain number of loans, and so on. The marks along the bottom row (the X axis) might show the time toward that goal (i.e., days or weeks), and the marks along the column on the left (the Y axis) might show the level of achievement (i.e., the current number of sales, clients, or loan closings). Then, as employees add to that goal, move the marker or cartoon character accordingly. In some cases, employees may enjoy the competitive spirit that comes from showing individual achievement, such as by having a different-colored dot or character for each employee to show each person's contribution to that goal—which is often fun for employees involved in sales. Though if employees feel threatened by showing individual achievement in this way, only make this a group goal.

45. Say It or Don't Say It Contest

If you work in sales, customer service, or other field where you have a lot of contact with customers or other employees, a fun contest to keep people aware of what they are saying is to organize a "Say It" or "Don't Say It" contest. In the "Say It" contest, you choose a word or saying of the day, which is something that people might not normally say, but could work into a conversation, such as: "Waste not, want not," "Look before you leap," or "That's earthshaking." Then, the person who uses the word or phrase the most often wins a small prize, such as a gag gift or an office pool created by each person chipping in $1.

An alternative is to pick out a common expression that people shouldn't say, such as "you know," "super," or "fantastic." Then, each time a person uses that word, he or she is penalized a point or a small amount (say 25 cents). Then the person with the most points has to pay a fun penalty, such as treating everyone to drinks after work, or the funds contributed are used to buy something fun, like buying lunch or dessert for everyone.

46. Play Name Games with Your Co-Workers

For a change of pace, try playing with new names, give each other nicknames, or try a "What's My Name" game at an office celebration. As an example of how this works, Showtime, an entertainment company based in San Francisco, has a party every few weeks to build team morale and pride, and help the staff of about twenty people unwind. At these parties, they began a tradition of giving people new names. They even began a tradition of officially knighting people with their new names at company dinners, and sometimes used humorous names like "Sir Loin of Beef."[3] Similarly, you might dub people with new names, either ones that they choose for themselves or ones that others suggest for them. These new names could be used at office celebrations—or every day, if people like their new names enough.

As an icebreaker to get people mixing if you have a large employee pool, you can use a variation of the "What's My Name?" game, which I used myself at a Bad Bosses party, designed to launch my book *A Survival Guide for Working with Bad Bosses*. In the game, you place a sign with the name of a well-known or famous person on each person's back, and then everyone goes around asking questions—such as: "Am I alive?," "Am I a woman?," or "Was I in politics?"—which can be answered with a yes or no. The idea is to try to guess the name on their back. Others respond by truthfully telling them the answer—or saying if they do not know. You can adapt this to your office or industry, such as by using names of people you work with or who are in the same business, as long as they will be generally known to everyone participating in the game.

47. Share Success Tapes

Many people are involved in all sorts of success programs, from workshops based on Rhonda Byrne's *The Secret* to Dale Carnegie motivational programs. So why not share the wealth? You might invite people to share their tapes or CDs during the lunch hour, after work, or even at an occasional meeting at work if management approves. Then, devote each session to one or two tapes or CDs, and as appropriate, participate in the exercises suggested on the tape as a group or have a discussion about the ideas presented, led by the person who brought the tape or CD.

48. Let People Brag

People really enjoy it when they have a chance to show off and brag about what they have done, so provide a forum for them to do so—during meetings, parties, lunches, or special celebrations to acknowledge what people have done. Invite people to share their latest achievements and activities in their work. And just so those who don't have any recent successes or highlights to share have something to contribute, invite people to share about their memorable and humorous personal experiences, too. This sharing makes a good opener for a meeting—perhaps after a humorous opener if you use one—or it can be done during the meeting. For example, the board of a Women's Business Group Network I belong to—the East Bay Women in Business Round-table—starts off their agenda with an overview of what is planned for the meeting. Then, after a few opening remarks by the meeting chair about what we hoped to accomplish, we would go around and share our personal successes and experiences for the past month.

49. Start Off Meetings with a Fun Opener

A good way to get everyone energized for a meeting is to kick things off with a fun opener. For example, invite people to do any of the following:

- Share a quick joke, particularly one related to the workplace or your industry.

- Ask people to complete a sentence that begins, "Wouldn't it be fun if . . ." or "The funniest thing I've seen at work is . . ."[4]

- Ask people to introduce themselves and then add something fun about themselves, such as: "My favorite way to have fun is . . .", "What I especially enjoy is. . . .", or "One of the most fun things I did this past week (month, on my vacation) is. . . ."

50. Add Some Humorous Touches to Your Meetings

Try bringing some humorous props to enliven your meetings, such as a clown nose, oversized glasses, or glasses with a big nose attached. Then, pick a word that no one should say, and every time anyone says that word, that individual has to put on the prop. For example, whenever someone in the meeting uses the word "serious" or a word meaning the same thing, that person has to wear Groucho Marx glasses or a hard hat. Other ideas for making meetings more fun—and perhaps making them run better—would be to hand out props to anyone who responds to another person's idea by immediately shooting it down rather than discussing it or tries to avoid responsibility by saying, "That's not my job."

51. Spice Up Your Meetings with Inspiring Stories, Art, or Videos

Consider beginning or ending your meetings with an inspirational story, display of art work, or video to put everyone in a better mood when you begin or end on an uplifting note. When you do this, you might appoint one person to bring in something inspirational to share at the next meeting or get together and perhaps rotate this role each time. Besides the inspiration and group bonding that results, the person who comes up with the inspirational idea will also benefit from their experience in researching the material to present and in facilitating the group.

52. Share Vacation Stories at Meetings

Would you like to know what others did on their vacations? Here's a way to spread the word in the office. Provide some time at the beginning or end of a meeting, when people who have been on vacation can briefly share what they did and even show photos or video clips. Or organize a party or celebration where everyone who has been on a vacation in the last few weeks or months (or since the last party) gets five to fifteen minutes to describe the highlights of their vacation, and if they have photos or videos, they can pass them around or show them using a video or DVD player and screen. Use a shorter time if many people have been on a vacation; longer if only one or two people have vacations to talk about.

53. Keep a Camera or Video Recorder in the Office

If the company doesn't have a camera or video recorder on hand, you might create an office pool to buy an inexpensive camera. Or people can alternate bringing in their own cameras or video recorders and volunteer to be the camera person on call for that day or week, should anything noteworthy occur. You'll all be glad later on that you were prepared in advance to record fun times around the office. However, keep your photography to times when people would like their photos snapped. You don't want to use a camera to take potentially embarrassing photos of people in the office, which wouldn't be much fun for them.

54. Create a Funny Photo Exchange with Other Employees

Here's a way to liven up office parties and celebrations with a little photo magic. This can be done with scissors and glue or some computer manipulations using Word, Photoshop, Paint Shop Pro, or other program. Start with some head shots of the people in the office, such as passport photos, or take some photos yourself. Preferably get photos where the images are about the same size and the person is looking forward, or almost forward.

Then, you can cut up the faces into slices and rearrange these, such as in the opener for the TV show *Ugly Betty*, where there is a collage of changing images of faces until Betty's full face finally appears. Or you can try pasting the faces onto different bodies, which you can obtain by cutting out photos from magazines and newspapers. For instance, paste one face onto the body of an astronaut to say that this person is really flying high. Put another face onto the body of a race car driver to humorously suggest that this is someone who drives a little too fast. Or if you think your boss is a real champ, put his or her face on the body of a champion boxer, as one employee of Bank of America did.[5]

55. Put Up Paper and Invite Others to Share Ideas and Images

If you have a door to your office or can requisition a nearby wall, you can put out some chart or construction paper for people to add their comments, short poems, cartoon favorites, and the like. Instead of evoking their comments with collections of images and cartoons, you are inviting people to use their creativity on an open canvas, so they can write or draw whatever they want.

I went to a New Year's party where the host did something like that. He put up long strips of wrapping paper along the stairs and hallways of his small apartment, attached some colored markers to each wall with a long cord and tape, and invited people to write whatever they want. "Just stick to the theme— what success means to you. Then, go to it." The result, toward the end of the party, was that the sheets of paper were covered with hundreds of comments, along with pictures torn from newspapers and magazines of images of success, such as big houses, huge cars, celebrities draped in bling, and a peaceful mountain stream by a cozy wooden cabin.

These invitations to comment and draw can also be a good way for you and others to express your feelings and frustrations about anything that is bothering you at work, though in a humorous good-natured way. For example, if people are feeling burned out from working overly long hours, a cartoon of a clock with tangled up hands might be a funny way to express that feeling.

56. Create a Humorous Video to Welcome Newcomers

If you or someone else likes using a video camera, you can create a fun video to introduce new hires to the job—or use them to train people in some office procedures. This might be an ad hoc kind of video you do on your own time—a little like a short YouTube effort. Or if you want to do this as a serious endeavor on company time, get a buy-in from management or your HR department. But before you start pointing the camera, plan out what you want to do and write a short script or guidelines to follow. Then, take a little time to rehearse some basics so people have a general idea of what they are going to say or do. Decide if you want to ask questions to which the people on camera will respond. After that, you're ready to roll. Just turn on the camera and sound, point, shoot, and start the action. Later, you can use a video editor to pull out the scenes you want to use and edit the video together. Aim for segments just a few minutes long, and put them together for, at most, a fifteen- or twenty-minute video, which is a good length, particularly if it will be used as an introduction or basis for further discussion. You'll find a wide selection of digital video cameras at your local camera, electronics, or computer store, and many computers already have editing software built in. If not, pick up an editing software program, such as from Roxio or Adobe.

57. Turn Gift Exchanges into a Chance to Be Creative

Does your office have a holiday gift exchange? Here's a way to add a creative fun twist. In the usual Secret Santa exchange, everyone secretly picks a name of the person they are going to give a gift to from a hat, bag, or box of names (and if you get your own name, throw it back). But instead of just buying an ordinary gift, you have to buy or create a gift, such as an ornament, mask, or small picture that evokes that person.[6] Then, display these objects around the office and everyone can try to figure out which gift goes with which person. It's a lot of fun to select or make these objects. Also, this is a great way to learn more about others in the office, especially about the person you have made the object for, since you have to learn more about that person and what he or she likes.

58. Create an Employees' Trivia Game

This can be a wonderful way to help employees get to know each other better and have fun at the same time. Start by giving employees some questions to answer about their background, including where they come from, their favorite activities and hobbies, descriptions of their families, amusing anecdotes, and any other information they want to include about themselves. Ask them to write one bit of information per card and mix up the cards. Give employees about twenty minutes to write up these cards either by hand or by typing up the answers on a computer. (If you are using a computer, create a table with a 3 × 3 matrix, write the answers in each of the nine boxes, print out the answers on card stock, and cut up the cards.) Then, using a trivia game board, have players roll the dice, and instead of asking a trivia question, an employee has to draw a card until he gets someone else's card. Then, he has to read that card aloud and guess which employee wrote it. If correct, the employee gets to move ahead on the trivia game board; if not, the employee who wrote the card identifies him- or herself, and the first employee remains where he is on the board. Either way, whether correct or not, all the employees learn more about each other and enjoy themselves along the way.

10

Organize Events, Celebrations, and Contests

The first two chapters of Part III have given you ideas for enjoying yourself more at work making the workplace more fun for yourself and others. But now, let's take it to the next level with ideas for organizing events, celebrations, and contests that everybody can enjoy. Depending on your office, this might involve working with your supervisor, the office manager, the owner, or the HR department. You might give them suggestions, or even give them a copy of this chapter.

59. Organize a Humorous Theme Contest or Event

The contest or event could feature almost anything. Volunteer or invite others to volunteer to be the coordinator and then plan a series of activities around a chosen theme. For instance, you might have a Best Hair Day and give out mock award certificates, a suggestion from Dave Hemsath and Leslie Yerkes.[1] Another possibility might be a Show Off Your Pet Day, where people bring in pictures of their pets, and you might have awards, such as the Best Dressed Pet, Funniest Costume, Ugliest Dog, Cutest Cat, and the like. A few other suggestions for events that might include awards and prizes are a Sing-Along Karoke Party, a Come as Your Favorite Celebrity day, a Bring Your Favorite Finger Food party, and a Poetry Slam competition, where you invite people to bring poems about your work.

60. Organize an Office Skit or Poetry Slam Party

This can be a fun way to add to a special occasion, like a celebration of a promotion, welcome for a new employee, or holiday party. You might organize a small group of employees to put on a humorous skit about something, such as a parody of office rules or funny conversations with customers. My publisher, AMACOM, puts on a skit twice a year at its semiannual Sales Conference, where a group of employees provides a humorous look at one of the books on that list for the sales reps.

Another idea is to invite people to bring in short poems about activities in the office for a poetry slam competition, with prizes offered to the person voted to have contributed the best or most humorous poem.

61. Have a Fashion Show

This might be combined with a Dress Up, Dress Down, or Costume Party day, where everyone shows off what they are wearing and then other employees or a panel of judges vote on who gets the prize.

Another approach is to have people wear their favorite or newest outfit for the day and parade down the hall or around the office like fashion models on the runway in New York, Paris, or London. You might add music, an emcee, and build up the excitement and drama of the occasion. Then, as employees show off their fashions, they might take off jackets, scarves, hats, or accessories, just like the models do in fashion shows. Meanwhile, the emcee or another employee could act like a commentator or reporter sharing the news about the fashion show. Everyone can vote for someone other than themselves who they think has made the best showing, based on not only what they are wearing but also their flare in showing it off.

This approach might also be used if your office is considering possible uniform choices—and if they want input from the staff. Then, a few employees might be selected to demonstrate the different choices, and others vote for their favorite choice.

62. Devise a Scavenger Hunt in the Workplace

If you have people at work who like to create puzzles, this could be a unique experience that helps people learn about the job, show off what they know, or discover what they don't. It can make a fun lunch break or after-hours party. Or a receptive boss might allow some time off for this, since it's all about work and teamwork. To set up the game, choose a series of objects to be located around the workplace and perhaps include a mark on them (like a sticker with a big "X" or a smiley face with a big grin) to show that this is the correct object. Then, write up a funny or mysterious clue, such as: "Illuminates some of the brightest ideas in the office," for a lamp in the conference room. Organize people into teams of two or three; give them a list or cards with clues on them; and invite them to race to come up with as many correct objects when the scavenger hunt ends, say in an hour. Participants score 1 point for each correct object; lose 1 point for each incorrect object; and the winning team gets a small reward—anything from a certificate or ribbon to individual coupons for a dinner for two at a local restaurant.

63. Organize a Peak-Performer Competition

Often competitions are organized between two, three, or more sales teams, depending on the size of the sales force. Then, the team with the highest sales during a particular sales period (monthly, quarterly, annually) wins a bonus or reward, and may be honored at a special dinner or celebration. For example, at the Fraser Paper Company, the salespeople, who are divided into two teams, have an annual Steak and Beans dinner, where the winners get the steak and the losers get the beans.[2] But such competitions can involve any division or department in a company, or be set up as a competition between departments, based on who contributes the most to the company in some way. As long as you can measure team, department, or division contributions, you can reward whoever performs the best and offer rewards and bonuses accordingly. And provide rewards to individuals who shine as well.

64. Invite Meeting Leaders to Create an Event

To make cross-departmental/divisional meetings more interesting, try letting different people or departments in the company lead them, and invite them to include a special presentation to share information about what they are doing. Some possibilities include:

- Creating a dramatic PowerPoint presentation, including photos, graphics, animated cartoons, and pulsating transitions. This makes it more entertaining than just listing an outline of key topics to be presented.

- Putting on a skit to play out what kind of work people do in their department.

- Using a talk-show format in which one person interviews others about their work a la Larry King.

65. Have a Diversity Day or After-Work Celebration

If you have people from different ethnic groups and cultural traditions in your workplace, this can be a great way to promote cultural understanding. These can be variously organized as a weekend or after-work event, at lunch, or at the end of the work day. One way is to give over each event to people from a particular ethnic or cultural group and invite them to share their customs and culture in their own way. For example, they might bring in some native dishes, play some of their music, read a poem or excerpt from a book about their culture, bring some examples of arts and crafts, put on a skit in costume, and otherwise share about their customs. They might also invite questions from others.

An alternative way to have a diversity event is to have people from different cultures bring examples of their food and art and either do a brief presentation or share informally with others about their culture. Use whatever approach works best for you based on the size of your workplace and the number and variety of people from different cultural groups. Living in the Oakland area, which has one of the most diverse populations in the nation, I've been at a number of such events that have been organized in different ways—and they have all been fun opportunities for learning about and celebrating diversity.

66. Organize a Creativity Workshop or Day

Here's a fun way to get everyone's creative juices going; it might be a program at a staff meeting or used as part of an afternoon gathering or even be turned into a Creativity Day. It's a great way to promote teamwork, too. The idea is to give team members a collection of objects; then each group has to come up with ways to use all of these objects together. I participated in an exercise that was described as a "survival game" in a management graduate seminar. The object was to take a collection of thirteen objects given to each team—and determine the priority of these objects for survival and explain why. The game assumed the team had arrived at an island in a rowboat with only the wet clothes they were wearing and this collection of objects. The objects included a compass, box of matches, first aid kit, a tarp, a canteen, furry hiking boots, and other items that I only hazily remember. Then, we had a half hour to come up with our choices, and afterwards, each team announced its list and reasons and the instructor explained what the most common rankings were and what a team of experts said were the best choices.

You can probably easily obtain a copy of this island survival game or something like it or create your own creativity exercise by choosing a half-dozen to a dozen objects. Give each group the same objects and invite them to figure out how to best use these together to create a novel product, marketing campaign, or invention. Then, after each group gets a half hour (or less) to come up with what they want to do, ask each team to talk about what they came up with and why they think it's such a great idea. Later, teams can vote on which idea they like best—other than their own—and say why. You might provide a small prize or ribbon for the winner and perhaps include other smaller prizes or ribbons for the second- and third-place winners.

67. Create a Match-Up Game to Help People Learn About Each Other

A fun way to both break the ice and get people to learn more about each other is playing a match-up game. There are various ways to do this.

- Have people bring their baby pictures, mix them up, and then hold up one at a time. Each person secretly votes on whose baby picture it is, using an erasable slate marker or a sheet of paper. Then, after everyone votes, reveal which picture belongs to which adult, and each person scores a point for a correct choice. The person with the most points wins, and you can provide an appropriate reward for the winner.

- Ask everyone to bring in a picture of their dog or a picture of a dog they would like to own. Then, as above, mix them up, hold them up one at a time, and have everyone secretly vote on the owner of the dog. Score as above for a correct vote, with the winner the person with the highest score.

- Use other match-up games, where people bring in a photo of something they own or would like to own, such as:

  ○ Their car

  ○ Their house

  ○ Their favorite hat

  ○ You name it

68. Have a "You Dream It" Event

Invite people to bring in one to three pictures of something they would really like to have or have happen. People can bring in a picture of anything they want, from an image of someone living a successful lifestyle to a picture of someplace they'd like to go to a picture of a product they want to own. For a series of rounds, people can bring additional pictures and use one per round. Pictures can come from newspaper or magazine articles, news stories, home photos, or other sources. People can glue them to cards, cardboard, or cover stock paper if they wish.

As above, everyone turns in a picture (they can put them in a grocery bag or other container or the facilitator can mix them up). Then, each person reaches in and takes out a picture and secretly writes down whose picture he or she thinks it is. If you get your own, either throw it back and pick again, if you can do this without revealing that it's your picture, or pretend it isn't and write down a guess—though you can't score a point for selecting yourself. Every correct guess is worth 1 point, and the person with the highest score wins.

69. Organize a Murder Mystery Game

This is a fun way to inspire teamwork and help people bond with one another. You can get a boxed game in a store to help you do this—or go to a local club that has a murder mystery game party. I went to one of these recently at a restaurant in L.A., where the victim, killer, and suspects were sprinkled around at the tables. The actors played out the game between courses, while the rest of us tried to look at what they were doing or wearing for clues. If you set up such a party, one approach is to put people in a department or division or who have to work together in the same group to encourage teamwork. Another approach, if you want to increase teamwork across departments or divisions, is to mix people in with others they don't know very well. In larger companies, you might combine people at tables based on the type of work they do, such as all sales people, all tech people, all account managers, and so on. Besides promoting teamwork and bonding, the game is also good for inspiring some friendly rivalry between groups, which can carry over into the workplace and spark increased productivity.

70. Have a Rewards-and-Recognition Party

Giving out rewards and recognizing accomplishments can be another way of having fun while increasing teamwork and creativity. Besides recognizing and rewarding individuals, you can promote team spirit with rewards to groups that have performed well—which can inspire continued high performance from

everyone in the future. While certificates, gifts, and financial rewards can be fine, you can add even more oomph to the occasion
by turning it into a time of real celebration. Some ways to do
this include providing a catered buffet or potluck, having an
emcee to make the announcements, accompanying the honors
with music, or even having someone dress up in costume for
the occasion (for example, if the event is around Christmas, the
reward giver could dress as Santa Claus; if it's around Halloween, he or she could dress up as a good witch or wizard; or if it's
just an ordinary workday, he or she could dress up as a well-
known celebrity known for being successful, such as Donald
Trump).

71. Create a Work Trivia Contest

Say you have to organize a training session for co-workers or
new hires. One way to make learning fun is to create a trivia
competition where people score for correctly answering questions about work. Prepare a series of questions and type them
on a series of cards. (One way to do this is to create a 3" × 3"
matrix in Microsoft Word, type a question on each of the nine
cards in the matrix, print these out on colored cover stock, and
cut out the cards.) Make as many of these as you can. Mix up
the cards and pass them out equally to each person or team.
Then, each person or team in turn reads their question aloud,
answers it, and if correct, gets a point. An alternate way is to
turn this into a race, where you turn up each card in turn and
invite participants to call out the answer. The first to answer
correctly gets 1 point, and anyone who calls out a wrong answer
loses 1 point. You can keep score on a score sheet, or create a
simple track board on a piece of cardboard. Participants can keep
score by moving their own marker, which can be chosen from
assorted office supplies, such as paper clips, rubber bands, eras-
ers, thumb tacks, and push pins.

72. Celebrate National Humor Month

Yes, there really is such a National Humor Month you can celebrate, and when else would it be but April? It was established in 1976 by Larry Wilde, the Director of The Carmel Institute of Humor, who has written over fifty books on humor. As he describes it on his website, National Humor Month is "designed to heighten public awareness on how the joy and therapeutic value of laughter can improve health, boost morale, increase communication skills and enrich the quality of one's life."[3] He picked April because it is often a bleak, grim, and stressful time of year since taxes are due on the 15th; he also chose April because it begins with All Fool's Day—a day that has sanctioned frivolity and pranks ever since the 1500s.

So think of special events or activities you might organize to help celebrate this month, such as dressing up in costume, having a humor party, or doing any of the other fun activities described in this book. Since you are tying these activities to National Humor Month, you should link whatever you are doing to this occasion, such as by creating National Humor Month awards. For instance, at a humor party or other celebration, give out humorous certificates, such as to "The Funniest Employee," "The Biggest Humorist," "The Employee with the Most Humorous Haircut," "The Employee with the Most Humorous Clothes," or "The Employee with the Biggest Grin." And if you wish, add some gag gifts as awards, or perhaps give the winners a humor book, such as one by Larry Wilde, since he was the National Humor Month founder.

73. Use Humorous Gifts for Office Celebrations

Want to liven up festivities when you are celebrating someone's birthday or achievements? Besides any serious gifts and rewards, add some humor. You might use funny work-related books, such as *The Joy of Work: Dilbert's Guide to Finding Happiness at the Expense of Your Co-Workers*, a tongue-in-cheek book of funny stories and Dilbert cartoons about finding humor in work in the trenches. Or you could include some humorous gift and toy items, such as a bad boss doll or a CEO who spouts funny phrases, like "Fire the goons"—items I found both on a Website featuring boss and moneyman dolls (www.happyworker.com) and in a sale rack at a second-hand store.

74. Find Novel Ways to Recognize Employees

Everyone loves to be recognized and honored for something. So find additional ways to celebrate selected employees, in addition to the usual times for recognizing people, such as birthdays, promotions, and anniversaries (of joining the company). For example, if someone has achieved something notable off the job, from getting engaged to getting married, from having a baby to writing a book or running a marathon, celebrate that event. Give that employee a gift (it could be a humorous gift as previously noted) at a weekly staff meeting or lunch-time party. Or do something fun, like turn out the lights and bring in a muffin with a glowing candle. You can even create a song or skit recognizing the achievement. And if the boss has done something for which everyone is especially appreciative, organize a celebration to honor the boss.

One way to continue this tradition is to have a fun-events committee to plan such events each month or quarter and select the employees to be honored. That group can then organize the events. And what if someone on the committee deserves to be recognized? Others in the group could plan such an event in secret as a surprise celebration—or someone not on the committee could set up a satellite group just for the one celebration.

75. Develop a Share-the-Wealth Reward Tradition

As they say, "to share the fun, give it away." The give-it-away approach is a way to share the honors in recognizing others and promoting teamwork. Here's how it works. You plan a celebration to honor someone for an accomplishment. Then give them two gifts—one for themselves and a second one for them to give to another employee who they feel gave them the most support in whatever they did. Or give everyone a gift and ask them to give it away to someone else they felt was especially worthy in supporting them or the company. Then, as the person gives a gift to another employee, he or she should briefly say why he or she feels that person deserves the honor. It's a process that should leave everyone glowing. Should you see anyone is being left out, have some extra gifts on hand, so the party organizers or coordinators can give that person a gift, too.

76. Establish an Employee Recognition Wall

Think of this space as like the "Head of Household Room" in *Big Brother*—a place where the winner of the weekly Head of Household competition gets to show off with personal items from home, like pictures with friends and relatives. While you can use it to select and feature the employee of the month, you can also use this as a place to feature personal items from everyone if the bulletin board, series of bulletin boards, or wall space is big enough. Invite whoever is featured—or everybody—to bring in their personal photos, including pictures of their home, family members, holiday outings, kids. Suggest that people bring in other fun things, such as drawings by their kids, favorite recipes, or blue ribbons or recognition certificates they have achieved in their hobbies off the job.

77. Submit Creative Ideas for New Products, Services, or Logos

Here's an idea that can be a win-win for owners, managers, and employees—inviting employees to submit their ideas for new products, services, or logos, with a reward or bonus for the winners with the best ideas, and even bigger rewards and bonuses for those whose ideas are used. To kick the submission process off, let employees know the types of new products or services the company is looking for, or tell them what kind of logo the company is looking for (i.e., a company logo or a logo for a new product or service) and then invite them to send in their submissions to a contest coordinator. Afterwards, the submissions might be sent to the company owner or managers to choose the best entries. Then, you might celebrate everyone who has submitted a suggestion with a party where you show off all the submissions and conclude with a ceremony to honor the best entries. You can use various options to judge them: you act as the judge, create a panel of three other employees to be judges, have your supervisor or company owner act as the judge, or have everyone vote for someone other than themselves.

78. Put On an Annual Humorous Awards Party

This could be a way to recognize both serious and humorous achievements, such as best sales performance, most creative design, and fastest production time on the one hand and categories like best excuse, messiest office, or employee with the worst customer. As an example of this approach, Laura Simonds of Davies Black Publishing worked with a previous employer who had an annual "Sweet and Sour Awards," which was organized like the Academy Awards, with prizes given to the best in a series of categories. As she describes to Dave Hemsath and Leslie Yerkes, employees could suggest a category and recommend a winner, who would receive either a sweet prize like ice cream or a sour prize like pickles.[4] One of the keys to keeping the event fun was to keep the humor lighthearted, so no one was intentionally hurt by the jibes. Similarly, you can use any number of award show formats and come up with any number of categories that fit your own organization.

79. Put On a Surprise Party for a Special Occasion

This can variously be a way to celebrate an employee's special achievement (and don't do this repeatedly, or the party will lose its surprise and it will become an office tradition). Find a reasonable way to get the honored guest out of the building—such as sending him or her on an errand or having another employee take the person out to lunch, and then be ready when the person returns to gather together or leap up from your desks to yell "Surprise!" After that, you can incorporate any of the other elements that make for a great party at work, such as skits and humorous awards.

The surprise can include a special gift (with money collected in an office pool), such as a dinner for two at a local restaurant or a massage at a local spa. Or perhaps you can offer an even more grandiose kind of award like a two- or three-day vacation if you can get management to contribute—and some will because of the increased morale building and productivity that such fun activities generate.

80. Start a Secret Santa or Gift Raffle Tradition

While Secret Santa gift exchanges typically occur at Christmas, they can be organized to happen at any time. So can gift raffles. The way a Secret Santa exchange works is that everyone who is participating brings a small wrapped gift (typically under $10) and places it in a big bag or box. In some cases, people will draw the name of the person they are giving that gift to in advance— and then will include a card for that person on the gift. Or people can just put in their gift. Then, everyone in turn pulls out a gift— and either gives it to the designated person on the card or keeps the gift for himself. Afterward, everyone shows off their gift— and people are free to exchange their gifts, if desired, for something they like better.

In a gift raffle, each person contributes a small amount to a group pot (say $1) and puts their name on a raffle ticket or small card that is mixed up in a bag or bowl. Then, the winner of the raffle keeps the pot.

One of the groups I belonged to—the Citizen Police Academy Alumni Association—used to do both of these. At every meeting, they had a raffle where everyone contributed $1, and the winner got half, with the rest going to the organization. Then, at their annual holiday party, they had a Secret Santa gift exchange in which people drew the names of their Secret giftee in advance. Part of the fun was for people to try to figure out who was their Secret Santa.

81. Use Candy for Fun Prizes and Awards

The brand names for popular candy and candy bars can lend themselves to some fun prizes and awards at parties. For example, here are some suggestions:

- Use PayDay as a prize for someone in accounting or someone who has scored a financial coup for the company.

- Use Almond Joy for someone who is especially bright and cheery or who has done something fun.

- Use a Butterfinger bar to gently chide someone who has made some recent mistakes.

- Use Jaw Breakers for someone known for talking a lot or communicating well.

- Use Life Savers for someone who has been a lifesaver on a project.

- Use Red Hots for someone who seems especially hot and sexy.

- Use Snickers for someone who makes everyone laugh.

- Use Three Muskateers for a team of three people who have performed well.

You can think of other appropriate awards for different candy bars at your local grocery.

82. Throw a Theme Party

Still another way to spice up recognizing an individual or the success of a particular project is to add a theme to a party or invite people to come as their favorite whatever. For example, I once put on a "Come as Your Favorite Misdemeanor Party" when I worked in the criminal justice field to celebrate settling a ticket for jaywalking, and it was attended by a mix of lawyers, prosecutors, and others in the field. You can use any kind of theme you can think of—something related to your industry might be especially appealing. For example, a humorous theme party for a staff of employees in retail or the fashion industry might be to come as your "Worst Dressed Fashion"; or a theme party for people working with animals or in the pet industry might be a "Do You Look Like Your Pet" day, in which people bring photos of themselves and their pets.

83. Organize a Be-a-Kid-for-a-Day Event

This can be a fun break at work or a fun event to stage for a few hours after work or on a weekend for employees who want to attend. The way it works is to invite employees to bring in one or more toys—and if employees don't have anything at home, suggest they go to a local toy store or a store with a big toy department, such as Target, Toys-R-Us, Wal-Mart, or K-Mart. They should bring in things like soft balls, beach balls, Styrofoam fencing swords, plastic bats, Frisbees, Slinkys, stuffed teddy bears, plastic building blocks, crayons, butcher paper, and the like. Scatter everything around the room and invite participants to pick out whatever toys they want and start playing with them by themselves, but then involve others. You'll find that people really let go, relax, and have fun. Afterwards, invite people to share what they experienced playing by themselves and then ask people to observe what happened when they join others to play together. Later, you can leave a collection of these toys at the office, say in a cabinet in the lunch room, so employees can bring them out for spontaneous play sessions. Or invite people to bring them back when you or someone else in the office organizes another play day.

84. Invite People to Create Poems and Songs About Their Work

Even if people aren't particularly talented, providing a showcase for poems and songs created by employees can be a fun way to celebrate the end of the work year or some other occasion, like an office party. This could even be turned into a humorous competition, where there are awards not only for the best poem or song, but for the funniest, weirdest, most outrageous, shortest, longest, or any other categories you come up with. Provide some suggestions to get people started, such as "The Day the Computer Went Down," "The Launch of Project T," and "Why I Like My New Office," and then let people's creative juices flow. You can invite people to bring in their creations to the event or set aside about fifteen minutes before, during, or after a staff meeting so people can write up their thoughts.

85. Organize a Family Day

A family day is a good way to introduce your co-workers to your family and/or show your family what you do. Some possible family events include:

- Bringing your children to work.

- Bringing your spouse or significant other to work.

- Inviting family members to a company picnic or barbecue.

- Having family members attend or participate in a company talent show.

- Bringing a pet to work.

Any kind of family/work event can be both a bonding experience and a great source of fun. (Of course, you had better make sure your bulldog doesn't attack the boss's Chihuahua.)

86. Plan a Birthday or Anniversary Celebration

In a relatively small office or within a specific department you may want to celebrate individual birthdays or anniversaries. Each person brings in a treat (home-made or store-bought) and sets it out in the break room or outside the celebrant's office or cubicle. The honoree feels special and everybody enjoys a bit of fun and food before getting back to the workday. If you are in a large office, you might group all the birthdays, anniversaries, or other special occasions for the month together and then honor all the people at one event. Also, this can be a time to celebrate other special events, such as births, graduations, and off-the-job achievements.

87. Have a Contest to Find New Uses for Your Company's Products

Here's a contest that's sure to be a company pleaser as well as fun. Invite people to submit ideas, photos, or videos showing new ways of using your company's products or services, and offer prizes for the most creative idea. For example, say your product is Jell-O. Some creative uses might be anything from whipping up unusual-looking desserts to using Jell-O as a lubricant to open up a stuck door. The entire group can vote on a winner, who will receive a small gift, and there could be bonuses if any of the ideas end up in company advertising or marketing campaigns for new ways to use existing products or services.

88. Organize a Special Event with Competitive Races

You can always stage a humorous race ideally suited to the workplace and to a special occasion, such as National Humor Month. For example, as described by Dave Hemsath in *301 More Ways to Have Fun at Work*, one outdoor recreation center organized a Rat Race Steeplechase and Admin Antics event, in which the administrative staff moved through various departments while competing in a series of events, which included:

•   A Disk Drive, in which employees teed up a computer disk like a golf ball and hit it as far as they could with a driver.

- A Toss Your Boss competition, in which employees dressed a blow-up doll like a boss and tried to toss it as far as possible.

- A Telephone Dash, in which employees raced to answer a phone while holding a cup of "coffee" (really water) and jumping over and around various obstacles to see who had the most coffee in the cup at the end.[5]

In the same way, you might adapt some events to your own office layout.

89. Organize a Theme Party Featuring a Fun Place

This can be a fun way to boost morale, especially if you get management involvement.

Pick a theme and then decorate the office, dress the part, and bring in food that fits the theme. For example, Auto Glass Plus in Carrollton, Texas, has a Hawaiian Day, for which people come to work wearing aloha shirts and put on floral leis. The employees also come in over the weekend to decorate the office with a Hawaiian theme.[6]

Similarly, you might think of other places that are associated with fun for a theme day at work. Some possibilities include:

- A Down Under Australian party

- A Brazilian carnival

- A Mexican mariachi party

- A Polynesian luau

90. Organize a Come-as-a-Character Day

Another kind of theme party revolves around picking out a character to dress as and act like for the day. It's like having a costume party, except with a theme, which you can expand on in the food people bring or in the skits or music featured at the end. For instance, some possibilities might be:

- Bring back the 1920s, 30s, 40s, 50s, 60s, 70s, or some other decade.

- Come as your favorite movie character.

- Come as a rock star or celebrity.

- Come as a member of high society at a society ball (which means dressing up in tuxes and gowns).

91. Take Photos or Videos of Special Events

Whatever type of event you are organizing—from theme parties to celebrating birthdays, anniversaries, and other special occasions, you can make it memorable with photos or videos. So arrange for one or more people to bring their cameras or video recorders to take pictures, and afterwards you can post photos on the wall, make copies for employees, or post videos on Websites or YouTube where everyone can view them.

Consider putting the photos in a photo book or scrapbook too, which employees can create on their own—or have a photo book or scrapbook for the office, perhaps kept in the lunch room, where it is easily accessible to anyone in the office.

92. Conduct a Brief What-Would-You-Enjoy Survey

Besides using the ideas suggested here, you might circulate a brief survey at your workplace to see what people would most like to do at an office party or what kinds of recognition awards they would most like to get. When David Hemsath and Leslie Yerkes did a survey for their book *301 Ways to Have Fun at Work*, they came up with a Top Ten list of people's favorite recognition gifts. The favorite was a coffee mug, preferably with a cartoon on it; followed by T-shirts, dinner, lunch or breakfast out, gift certificates to almost anything, balloons, tickets to a sports event, books, plaques and trophies, popcorn tins or fruit baskets, or gag gifts.[7] But you may find different opinions in your own workplace when you query people yourself. In conducting the survey, it helps to start with a list (such as the one here plus your own ideas) and ask people to rate them from 0–5, based on how much they would like that event or award. Then, ask them to add their own suggestions. Afterwards, tally up the results and use that as a guide to planning your next parties and award-giving ceremonies.

11

Take Your Fun Outside of Work

Not all fun activities with your co-workers have to take place in the workplace. Besides having fun at the office, you all can have some truly fun times off-site. This final chapter of Part III gives you some ideas on taking your fun outside.

93. Trade Off Your Hours So You Can Have Some Extra Time for a Party

If you've got a job where flexibility is possible, then try to work out arrangements where people can work longer hours one day so they can get some extra time off for a party—either at the office or in some fun place nearby. Or perhaps even use the extra hours for an excursion to someplace special, if others at work agree on what to do. For instance, I know some people who organized a day at the races, with the approval of their boss, by working longer hours for several days during the week. Then, their reward was getting off early on Friday, so they could get to the race track.

94. Organize a Home Party for Other Employees

You can have an office party outside the office, using any number of the techniques described for throwing a great office party. If one person especially likes to have parties, put that person in charge of having a party in their own house and create a committee to help out. Or consider rotating the job of host or hostess from employee to employee and have a party every two to six months. Invite people to indicate what times they would prefer (i.e., afternoons, 6–9 P.M., 7–10 P.M.) and what days (weekends, weekdays, Monday, Tuesday, etc.). Then pick a time and day that seems to work best for the most people.

To make it easier for the host, turn the party into a pot luck, and to prevent a scenario where you end up with too many desserts, beverages, main courses, or whatever, ask people to write down on a list what they plan to bring. If you're overfull in one category, steer that person into bringing something else where you are so far undersupplied. Use some icebreakers or quick-to-play communication games to help get everyone warmed up and mixing. Then, go enjoy yourself.

95. Have a Party at a Local Restaurant

This makes an ideal after-work gathering—as well as a way to check out the local restaurants. A good way to find out the type of foods most people prefer is with a quick survey (i.e., "Write down your three favorite types of food"), and then vary the type of cuisine as well as the restaurant. After you set the date, ask people to RSVP a few days in advance, and reserve a table for that many people, plus allow a few extra spots for last-minute drop-ins. If people can't make it at the last minute, ask them to let you know, so you can advise the restaurant accordingly. Besides using the time to socialize freely, you can also combine the dinner with a few other special events, such as funny or serious awards to recognize employees for different accomplishments or a gift exchange (especially if the dinner is held near a holiday like Christmas or Valentine's Day).

96. Organize a Group Outing

An occasional trip to a special event can help to create a strong friendship network or family feeling on the job—providing a great boost for both morale and productivity. If these aren't already organized by management, you can easily organize your own. Pick the kind of event that will be popular among employees, such as a day at the races, a trip to a local baseball or basketball game, a picnic, a movie night, a trip to a local winery or brewery, or a day of fishing or outdoor games at a nearby park.

To find out what people like before you start planning, write down a list of possibilities, invite people to add their own, and ask people to rate the items on their list from 0 (no way) to 5 (sounds great; I'd love to come). Then, combine the items on the lists, tally the number of votes, and use these lists to choose what the group would most like to do for a trip. You also might get written feedback on the time and day when people would prefer to do this. Besides circulating a survey or list for input and ratings, you can use a fun suggestion box to get input, or perhaps put up a blackboard or whiteboard in the conference room or lunch room, and invite anyone to add their ideas of what to do as a group.

Once you've chosen an event, make the necessary arrangements, such as reserving tickets and collecting advance payments, and plan any special activities you expect to have at the event, such as icebreakers, communication games, and activity/skill games. Also, arrange for other people to help out in hosting the event or facilitating various activities. Should the event prove popular, consider turning it into a monthly, quarterly, semiannual, or annual event.

97. Participate as a Group in a Local Race

Some communities have humorous races. For example, in the Oakland area, there are Bathtub Regattas (where local groups compete by turning their bathtubs into wacky-looking boats), Chair Races (where participants race along holding up one person in a chair), and even Toilet Bowl Races (where participants turn a toilet bowl into a kind of racing car). Find out what kinds of fun races are run in your area. Then see who wants to sign on to participate.

Likewise, you can organize your own wacky race and turn it into a fun office tradition. Just about anything can become fair game for a race, from kites and wooden make-it-yourself race cars to office furniture (preferably on wheels). Select wacky prizes, too, to suit the offbeat humor of whatever the race.

98. Put on a Sales Party or Product Party

In many companies, employees have side businesses where they represent different companies that put on sales or product parties, such as multilevel, network marketing, and party planning companies. Any of these individuals would be delighted to put on such a party, say at lunch or after work. Or perhaps you could combine two or three people with different or complementary product lines, so you have a potpourri of offerings. All sorts of products make great candidates, such as Mary Kay makeup demonstrations for women employees, food-tasting parties from companies featuring food products, and demonstration of cooking equipment, toys, fashion items, or health-care lines. Ask people what kinds of products they might like to show and then turn over the lunch hour or after-work gathering to them.

99. Create an Auction or Fund-Raiser for a Worthy Cause

Is there some worthy cause that people in the office want to get behind? You can set up an auction or fund-raiser to come up with funds to contribute in the name of your office or group. One way to do this is to choose a cause at a regular office meeting—or send out a memo inviting people to a luncheon or after-hours group to participate in this—and be sure to give those who don't want to participate the ability to opt out. You don't want people to join in because of peer pressure; you want people who really support the particular cause you have adopted. Then, choose something that inspires the group. This can range from collecting funds to help someone at the office who is having personal troubles to donating to a local, national, or even global cause, such as raising money to support a foreign family or save the rain forests in Brazil.

Once you choose a cause, the next step is planning the auction or fund-raiser. One possibility might be to invite people to bring items they were planning to discard at home and have an auction for these items at work. Another possibility is to use some humorous items to bid for, such as one company that auctioned off their managers to the highest bidder at the annual holiday party and then donated the money (typically around $500) to several organizations for their annual food drives.[1]

100. Organize a Workout-Together Program

Want to stay in shape? Organize a workout session for others who are interested during your lunch hour or after work. You might go to a local health club or gym together (you might even qualify for lower rates by going as a group) or bring in some equipment and find a room where you can exercise at work. For example, bring in some weights and take turns lifting weights. Do knee bends. Do aerobics or Pilates moves. Bring in a radio so you can play music or an aerobics tape. Or if it's a nice day, do a group jog or power walk around your block.

101. Find a Fun Setting in Which to Have Your Meeting

You don't always have to meet in a conference room or office. A good way to get everyone relaxed and to expand thinking, especially for meetings where you want to encourage new ideas, is to find a fun setting in which to have your meeting. Some possible places to meet might be:

- At a nearby park, particularly one that has a picnic area or quiet meadow that's idea for a small meeting. For example, I've been to some meetings in Oakland at a duck pond, large lake, and a picnic campsite in a wooded grove.

- By a pool (and if so, be sure to invite participants to dress casually and come ready to enjoy the sun—or bring a large hat if they want to be in the shade).

- At local sites of interest, such as in a historic house, where attendees can visit the attraction before or after the meeting. Even a "haunted house" might make a suitable location for an October meeting before Halloween.

- At a holiday celebration, such as on the porch of a house during an Easter egg hunt or on a turkey farm for Thanksgiving.

PART IV

Expand Your Fun
Horizons

12

Explore New Possibilities

The key to bringing more fun into your life and acting in the spirit of play is being spontaneous, creative, and innovative. The fun spirit is associated with trying out and doing new things, exploring and being open to discovery, and otherwise experimenting with and embracing new possibilities. Besides finding new ways to bring fun into your workplace, described in Part III, you can look for ways to find new possibilities both on and off the job.

Finding New Activities

One way to bring more fun into your life is to try new types of activities and events you have never done before. Use the local calendar in your weekly or daily newspaper to discover possibilities. Just look for activities that are new and different for you— and that may involve pushing out of your comfort zone. Be open to experiment, so even if you don't initially like something, spend a little more time with it, because your attitude might change as you become more familiar doing something new.

Another source of new activities and events is the growing number of social connection services found on the Internet. An organizer starts the process going by setting up the Website and uses software to create the interface for members to sign up for activities. But then most of the content is provided by local event leaders or organizers, who dream up activities and invite others to sign up. These organizations can be a quick and easy way to create a social world for yourself outside of work, particularly if you need to have more of a life–work balance.

One example of this phenomenon is the LinkUp system, which has activities in about two dozen cities and regions, including groups in the San Francisco, Los Angeles, Miami, Las Vegas, Hawaii, Denver, Dallas, Minneapolis, and New York areas, and even globally, with groups in London, Paris, Vancouver, Toronto, Hong Kong, and Shanghai. (There will probably be even more by the time this book gets into print.) Activities feature everything from an investing club to games to scrapbooking to going to unusual events, like a fire dance.

Another is meetup.com, which has groups in about two dozen cities around the United States as well as a dozen groups in Canada and in dozens of countries. You just click on the city, put in the area where you want to join a group, see a list of upcoming activities, and sign up. While the organizers pay a small amount to create groups, it's free to participants, and you can try out a variety of new activities. For example, since I started commuting to L.A. about two months ago, I have quickly found groups there to do all sorts of activities: going to a costume party with a DJ in a private house in the Hollywood Hills, singing in a private room in a Korean Karoke bar, participating in a murder mystery dinner party, and going through a corn maze at a Harvest Festival at a local college. These are things I would have never found out about on my own and even if I had heard of them, might have been hesitant to go to myself. But within days, I was part of a network of people trying out new activities all over L.A.

These groups can be ways to enhance your work as well, such as if you want to get together a small informal focus group to react to a new product or service offered by your organization. Or you might use the networking power of these groups to find products or services you can use yourself. And you can easily set up your own groups based on your own interests. For instance, after meeting one woman at a party who had her own meet-up group for actors, I set up a salon for actors to bring clips of their work to show at a screening room in my building, so I can explore the possibility of producing a low-budget film. And since this woman already had the group of actors organized, I just had to provide a date and place for the event. So with little effort, I was able to quickly connect with the usually hard-to-break-into film industry.

Similarly, you might think of the various types of activities you would like to do, see if there is a linkup, meet-up, or other type of social networking group in your area, and check if anyone has already organized an activity you would like to participate in. If not, start your own group, announce an event, and see what happens.

Carving Out More Time for Yourself

Another way to try out new possibilities is to actually schedule time in your calendar when you will try out something new, much like you might schedule a regular appointment for work. It's like creating an appointment with yourself to allow yourself time to explore. Now, you may find it easy to cross such "appointments" off your schedule when work or other demands seem pressing, because you give those things a higher priority. But you should make upping your enjoyment a high priority, too. Then you'll keep these appointments with yourself once you make them, except when you really do have a serious emergency to deal with. This is a great way of creating a better work–life balance in your life—and it also helps you find ways to add more vitality to your life and keep yourself from feeling stale and un-motivated.

Figure out how much time you want to devote to trying out new possibilities and then note them on your calendar as a way of creating a new, more energized you.

Finding New Places for a Change of Scene

Changing your locale is another way to re-energize yourself. Not only should you try out new things but you should find new places in which to do them. To that end, it might be worth driving that extra half hour to go further out of your usual area in trying out new activities. For instance, if you live in one city, go to a neighboring city and join some groups there to expand your social life. Consider using a nickname or middle name when you participate in these activities; perhaps use a separate e-mail or phone number. The rationale is a little like creating an altar ego or avatar in a virtual world, such as Second Life, where you can participate in everyday activities on-line, from buying and sell-ing goods to creating businesses and socializing. But here you are creating a kind of second life for yourself in reality, where you can take off for a few hours and have a whole new set of social relationships somewhere else. Incidentally, this is not to advocate taking this new part of you so far that you step out on your ordinary obligations or betray your important relationships. It's more like taking minivacations from your everyday life, a little like kids taking off to a backyard playhouse, where they can create a new world for themselves for a brief time.

Another way to attain this second-life experience is to have a vacation home in another city, state, or country, which many people do, either by owning the home individually or as a time share. In fact, according to a Harvard University study, "Multiple Home Ownership and the Elasticity of Housing Demand," by Eric S. Belsky, Zho Xia Di, and Dan McCue,[1] about 6.8 million Americans own second homes (that's 6.5 percent of homeowners), with the peak among them being in their fifties and sixties, and about 5.5 percent have time shares, for a total of about 12 percent. The figures are about 6–8 percent for those in their thirties and forties. If you can't afford to buy, you can always rent a place on a short-term basis or possibly arrange for a home or apartment swap through various rental and home share services, which are easily found on the Internet today.

Then, you can use being in this new environment to help you feel more open to trying out new possibilities. At the same time, you can use the new technologies to work away from your usual home or office or even set up another working office, so you can easily work in either location. For example, you can set up a computer in your second home and take a CD or DVD or datastick containing any needed files along with you, or you can e-mail them to yourself, as well as bring or send any physical files and materials you need. You also can set up software so you can access your home computer from anywhere on the Internet.

For example, I recently set up an office in Santa Monica. For several years, I had been feeling that I wanted a change of scene, after working long hours juggling writing books and scripts with running a business connecting clients with decision makers in nearly a dozen industries. Though I tried for about two years to find someone to take over the business, I still hadn't sold it and felt it was too successful to just walk away from it. But it was a labor-intensive computer and Web-based business that involved ongoing customer contact. So what could I do? Finally, I came up with the perfect solution.

I found an apartment/office in a totally different environment—in the heart of downtown near the beach compared to living in a house in the hills of a medium-sized city in Oakland. I was able to set up a computer, printer, and scanner there, so I can easily take my business with me. At the same time, I began to establish a totally different business in L.A.—becoming a film producer and setting up a syndicated radio show, while joining assorted film industry and social networking groups. About every three weeks, I drive to L.A. for ten to twelve days. Rather than flying, which can involve long delays at the airport and traveling to and from the airport at either location, I simply drive—about six hours door to door. When I began the process, I figured that either this move would help me successfully enter the film industry or it would just be a way of taking a much-needed long vacation. So far, it has been working in both respects.

You may find that this kind of dual-city lifestyle is a way to cultivate new sources of enjoyment in your own life.

Choosing the New Possibilities for You

From finding new activities in your local events calendar to finding new places to try out new activities, you can discover lots of new possibilities to try out.

In some cases, you might want to previsualize what you are thinking of doing before you actually do it, to decide if this is something you want to pursue in reality—such as when you are contemplating a significant change. Or you might make the change in stages, so you gradually learn more about the new place, through one or more short stays, before you actually make a move. That's what I did before I decided to set up a satellite office/apartment in L.A.

First, I made a drive-through of the area, when I was in L.A. to meet someone for another purpose. I had decided that I wanted to be near the beach and the airport, since I liked the feeling of openness of the water and I would be going back and forth between two cities. So, as I drove around with those two criteria in mind, I imagined what it might be like to live in different nearby cities—Marina del Rey, Venice, and Santa Monica. (Interestingly, I felt the greatest sense of affinity for Santa Monica. Sometimes, you have to simply trust your intuitive or gut-level feelings.)

Among other things, I used visualization to see myself living in various places as I drove around—from high rises to town houses to small houses near downtown. Then, I arranged for a few short trips in which I stayed in a hotel near the beach, so I got a greater sense of what it was like to live there. Finally, after I had made the decision to set up a satellite/apartment office there, I used my last stay in a hotel to look for places, using the local paper and a rental service. I targeted where I wanted to live based on certain criteria I had established: must be downtown on a main street, so I can meet with clients in an office-like setting; must be large enough, so I can set up a computer to run my business; must be in a secure building, since I will be out of town for several weeks each month; must be on a ground floor, since it will serve as an office as well as an apartment.

I visited several buildings to look at the apartments. I monitored the building I selected through their online Website until a ground floor apartment became available. Then I rented it. After that, with a copy of the floor plan in hand, I carefully visualized what the furnished apartment would look like, so I had a clear vision of what furniture I would need. The first day I arrived, I came with a sleeping bag and mattress. That way, I could stay in the unfurnished apartment while I shopped for furniture one day and arranged with a furniture assembly service to come in the next day to put everything together. Within a few days, the place I had visualized was put together. On the next trip about ten days later, I had all the computer, phones, and other equipment installed, so the office was ready to go. Meanwhile, besides setting up the office, I began going to events sponsored by the various film industry and social networking groups I had joined, so I increasingly felt settled and connected in this new environment.

I've described this process at length to illustrate that this is the kind of arrangement that anyone who wants such a second or parallel life can easily use. Just previsualize what you want to do, where you want to go, and what this new life might look like, and then take steps to implement your vision. It may turn into a parallel or new career plan, it may be more like a vacation where you are trying out something new and expressing new aspects of yourself, or it may be a little of both. It may be helpful to think of this as more of a vacation and, only secondarily, as a career change or expansion. That way, you can always see this as an enjoyable growth experience, whether the career change works for you or not. And, of course, you can always continue or extend the experience, or end it, when your lease or the time you committed to this change is up.

13

Make Travel Time More Interesting and Enjoyable

Whether you're commuting to work or traveling for business, you can use various techniques to make your travel time more interesting. These are techniques to use when you're not already doing work along the way, say on your laptop or in a notebook, and most of them are designed for when you're traveling on a bus or train or a passenger in a car—not for when you are driving. These ideas are adapted from my book *The Creative Traveler*.[1]

Make Your Ride More Interesting

If you're on a long ride, here are some creative alternatives to spice up your ride. Use any or all of them or create some of your own.

Imagine Yourself in the Setting

Instead of just watching the scene go by, add interest to what you are seeing by imagining yourself in the scene. Do this quickly as you are traveling past a scene. The process is like projecting yourself into a series of moving slides as they flash by.

For example, as you drive through the countryside, imagine yourself walking through it. If you pass some construction workers, feel what it might be like to be part of the gang. Or as you see people walking by, think what their daily lives might be like. Ask yourself a few quick questions, such as: Where are these people going? What kind of work do they do? What are they probably thinking or feeling now?

This technique helps you pay more attention, focuses your awareness, and helps you to see and experience more.

Create and Play Seeing Games

Another way to liven up your trip is to play "seeing" games in which you look for selected objects in your environment, and tally them up or check them off as you see them. You can do this yourself or with others you are traveling with. To add a competitive element in a group, race to be first to see various objects or to finish the list first.

To create this seeing game, work out a list of ten to twenty likely objects you may observe on your ride in advance. For example, say you are driving through open countryside; you might list things like: a farmer in the field, a wind catcher, a man on a horse, a cow. Then, watch for these objects. If you're doing this alone, check each one you see and see how long it takes you to complete the list or how many you can find within a certain time limit. With a group, tell people to call out when they see something. Keep playing until the time is up; then the player who has scored or checked off the most objects wins. Or set a certain number of objects as the goal (i.e., seven), and the first to see that many objects wins.

Play Travel Bingo

In this bingo-type game, your object is to spot certain letters or numbers on the sights you pass on the road, or on city buildings. You score by identifying a certain number of them to make up a word or arrange a series of letters or numbers in a row.

To set up the number version, create a series of cards with different random numbers in a list or in a 5 × 5 matrix, as in bingo, with a free space in the middle. Use only single numbers from 0 to 9, since it can be hard to get specific larger numbers.

As an alternative to creating all the cards yourself, suggest that everyone playing create their own list of numbers before you start the game. Then, as you travel, players should circle the numbers they see. As players pass signs with numbers (such as signs indicating the speed limit or distance from one town to another), they should check off the corresponding numbers. For example, if a distance sign indicates that it is 23 miles to the next town, each player who sees this can mark off a 2 and a 3. Or if players prefer, one player can call off these numbers for everyone else. This way, everyone will work with the same numbers, but look for different numbers or have different card layouts. However players set up the game, the first player to get the numbers he needs for his card is the winner.

In the letters version, create a series of word cards, like anagrams. Or have players create their own lists of short words, say four to five letters each. Suggest a theme—animals, plants, places, objects, actions—for these words. Then, players have to look for letters for their words on the signs or buildings they pass. In this case, however, they can only take a limited number of letters from each sign (such as one or two letters). You can do this alone to see how fast you can make words, or race with other players. With a group, players can take turns calling out a word they see for everyone else to work with, so everyone has the same number of words to use in looking for letters from them to match the letters on their card. As in the numbers version, the first player to get the letter she needs to complete her card wins the game.

Take Some Time to Write

Long rides can also be a good time to write up your memories or reflections of the trip or catch up on letters, whether you write them in longhand or on your laptop. (This is, of course, only for those who do not get carsick from reading in a moving vehicle.) Besides keeping an ongoing journal of what you have experienced you can record your current impressions. Writing down your experiences or impressions will help to make you more aware and able to experience more. If you review these impressions from time to time, your entries may give you even more ideas.

In recording your impressions, begin by jotting down your most immediate observations much like a reporter might recount what she is seeing. Then add your thoughts about what you observed, and comments about your feelings. Some people adopt this approach to use their trip as the basis for a thoughtful inward journey; others simply want to keep a day-to-day record of the trip. In either case, a long ride can be an ideal place to put down these thoughts.

Photographing While You Ride

Taking photographs on a trip can help make your ride more stimulating, as well as recording what you see along the way. It helps to have a camera that can take photos at a speed of at least 1/1000 of a second, because you can freeze-frame just about anything you pass with this kind of shutter speed. With a slower speed, wait for the vehicle to slow down or focus on long-distance shots. You may not get your best shots, because you are generally moving quickly and don't have much time to plan or frame your shot. So you may find stray trees and poles in your shot, because you can't control the exact moment when your shutter snaps as you move. But a percentage of your shots may still turn out to be really good, and regardless of the results, the process will help to make for a more interesting, exciting ride.

When you take photos, it's generally better to sit on the right side of the car, bus, or train, so you don't have to worry about traffic rushing by and spoiling your picture. If there are extra seats on the bus, find one where you can move freely from one side to the other. This way you can shift around when you see a good shot coming up on the other side. If you can, sit on the front seat next to the driver. This way, you can take pictures from the front and side windows.

Where possible, open the window and stick your camera or lens through the opening to avoid streaks and reflections from the glass in your picture. If you can't do this, try to find the clearest part of the window. Set your camera on automatic if you can to avoid having to change the exposure as you move rapidly from one setting to another. However, if you are in a situation where getting the correct exposure is difficult, because a great deal of light sky reflection will give you an underexposed picture, set your camera on manual, open up the aperture a bit to adjust for the extra light, and shoot at this preset speed. When you move to another location, you can either go back to automatic or reset your camera on manual for the next series of scenes.

Turn Your Stops into Miniadventures

When you stop for a few minutes on a long ride, make the best of this with a little planning. Find out in advance from the driver

192 of Expand Your Fun Horizons

where you are going to stop and for how long. Then, plan what you want to do and how much time you have for each activity.

For example, if you are going to stop for about ten minutes at a market, think about what you want to do there (i.e., take photographs, buy some souvenirs) and give yourself a certain amount of time for each task and decide what to do first based on what's most important to you. You might start off with two minutes of simply taking a 360-degree look all around you; then take two minutes of photos to record the scene; take about six minutes to purchase the souvenirs you want; and get back to the bus, van, or car in time.

Ask the Tour Guide Questions

If you take a tour while on a business trip to another city, state, or country, a long ride is a great time to obtain information from your guide on all sorts of topics not part of the regular tour. To do this, sit next to or within a few seats of the tour guide. You'll find many guides will be especially responsive to your questions, because they appreciate your interest in the area where the guide lives or works. If you ask personal questions (but not too personal) about the guide's background, the guide will usually be flattered by your interest.

Ask as many questions as you wish, as long as you feel the guide is being responsive and is giving you full answers, which indicate that he or she is pleased to answer. However, once you sense resistance, either because you have asked too personal a question or have started to overwhelm the guide with too many questions, stop your queries for a while.

Often guides know a great deal more about each place you are visiting than they give as part of a formal presentation to the group and usually are only too happy to share this information. Some good questions might be about the local population, major industries, what people do for recreation, the guide's opinions about events in the news (though be careful about choosing controversial events; this may lead to a more combative than fun discussion). In some cases, you may be able to stimulate an in-depth discussion, which may give better insight into what is happening in that area and how most people think.

In some cases, guides may be reluctant to respond, because they feel pressure to present an official and positive view of their city or country. So be sensitive to how much the guide wants to say on a topic, and shape your questions to stay away from taboo topics. You might also ask your guides for personal background information, such as how they happened to become guides, what they like about the job, what they did before, etc. Most guides enjoy telling you about themselves, and appreciate this personal attention.

Get More Out of Your Flight

An airline flight can be another opportunity to enhance your trip with creative travel techniques—or to increase your enjoyment of the typical things people do on flights: reading, listening to music, watching the movie, or having a meal.

Enjoy Your Music More

As you listen to music on your headset, take ten or fifteen minutes to experiment with listening techniques to achieve a more intense musical experience.

- See imagery as you listen.

- Create a musical scene or story in your mind.

- Experience the music as a sound sculpture existing in three-dimensional space.

- Let the music become a musical landscape.

- Create a dance for the music in your mind.

- Focus on experiencing the music at different parts of your body.

- Imagine the music as an energy flow pouring through you, and let it invigorate you.

The airplane is an ideal place to relax and experiment with these different experiences; as you listen, let yourself slip into this world of your imagination. In fact, if you're on a late-night flight when the lights are low and the hustle and bustle of serving drinks and food is over, these techniques are especially ideal. You can pay closer attention to this musical world and experience it more fully.

You can experiment with shifting from one musical environment to another by changing headset channels. Use one of the above techniques with music on one channel; after you have gotten into the experience, quickly shift channels, and continue your imagery or story from there. Take some time to leisurely adjust to the new rhythms and tonalities before moving on to something else or going back to the first channel.

You can also experiment with shifting back and forth between channels quickly. Spend a few seconds on each channel, long enough to get a picture, feeling, or sound landscape, and then switch. You'll find the experience is a little like looking at a series of constantly changing slides or hearing bits of songs for an album promotion. You may find the quick shifting of musical landscapes an exhilarating rush, because of the rapid change of pace and tone.

Imagine Yourself in the World Outside

This approach is similar to that described in the previous section on making your ride more enjoyable. However, your in-the-air view gives you a different perspective for trying out these techniques. Ideally, sit next to a window, preferably one with a completely clear view, not one that is over the wing.

Now imagine yourself outside the plane flying through the air. Feel yourself floating, drifting, and soaring. Experience the freedom and exhilaration of free flight. If there are no clouds, imagine yourself zooming through the air; experiment with moving ahead as fast as you can; then feel yourself floating slowly. Try looking down to see what's below, but concentrate on flying in the air.

Another approach is to imagine yourself on the ground you see below you, where you are walking, riding in a car, on a horse, sitting, or standing. However you see yourself, look around and experience the environment. Ask yourself questions to focus on different things, such as: "What am I doing here? Who else is here? What are the people like in this setting? How do I feel about being here?"

Writing as You Fly

Flying is another great time to do some writing. You can write in your journal, brainstorm to come up with creative ideas, make notes on the high points of your trip so far, or catch up on letters.

Brainstorming New Ideas

Flying can be an excellent time to come up with new ideas, especially on a relatively long flight, because there are few distractions for most of the flight, apart from a few comments by the pilot or flight stewards at the beginning of the flight and a brief break for meal service. So this is an ideal setting for brainstorming ideas. If you are trying to find new ideas—such as for launching a new project, setting future goals, or finding a solution to a problem at work—this might be the perfect place to do it. While brainstorming is often done in a group, you can easily brainstorm yourself, by just giving yourself the freedom to think as far outside of the box as you want, without censuring your thoughts.

Initially, come up with as many ideas as you can, without trying to be critical or judgmental. In the second stage of the process, you can decide which ideas you like and want to put into action by evaluating the ideas generated in the first stage. To help you remember your ideas, use a notebook or your laptop to write them down. For example, on several occasions, I used flying time to come up with ideas for new games. I set aside a half-hour for brainstorming, opened a notebook, and once ready to write, I opened my mind to any ideas for games. In whatever form these ideas came—a name, a theme, scenes of people playing games, mental pictures of game boards—I wrote them down. Later, I reviewed them, and chose a few for further development. Certainly, not all of these ideas were good, but that doesn't matter, because the essence of brainstorming is to quickly generate whatever ideas come to mind without trying to be critical. In the process, many ideas will be rejected. But some will be good and some may be *very* good, as I found when I sold some of the ideas I had first thought up during individual in-flight brainstorming. You may similarly find some great ideas, as well as having fun with the process.

Getting to Know Your Seatmate

Your seatmate on a flight can be a wealth of information and ideas. To get a conversation going, you may need to break the ice, since people generally fly (or take other forms of public transportation) with the expectation that they will not get into an extended conversation with their seatmate. But, once you break the silence barrier, you may find the person is eager to talk. If so, you can use this opportunity to get to know your seatmate and to find out about where he or she lives.

Start with small talk and sense if the person is open to conversing—and if this is someone you want to talk to. Brief remarks about the flight, the weather, or your destination are excellent. If you sense the person is receptive—indicated by such things as complete, detailed answers or return questions to you—ask more personal or background questions, such as "Where are you from?" or "What do you do?" Once you are both talking freely, you can shift the conversation to topics you are particularly interested in. It may help to think of yourself as a roving reporter seeking information on a topic. Imagine yourself interviewing your seatmate for the story.

When you seek to draw your seatmate into a conversation, be sensitive to whether the person really wants to talk and for how long. For instance, if your seatmate seems to be very busy— say he's a businessman writing a report on his laptop—a few pleasantries might be fine, but the person probably doesn't have time to talk, so don't push it. On the other hand, you may find someone your age, who is eager to pour out all his or her troubles to you. If you don't mind playing therapist or counselor, you might find this interesting and be able to help your seatmate as well. But if you find the conversation is weighing you down and you'd like to get out, find a diplomatic way to disengage. Say something like: "It's been interesting talking to you, but now I have to (catch up on my mail, get back to my book, write my report, etc.)." Or excuse yourself to go to the restroom; when you get back, explain that you have something you must do before the plane lands.

Experiment with Your Extrasensory Perception

If you are interested in ESP and have a willing seatmate, a flight can be a good time to experiment with this. To do so, take turns thinking of something, and have the other person try to mentally pick up what this was. Some likely possibilities for this process include: numbers from one to five, colors, nearby objects on the plane, cities along the route, etc.

Choose a category with a limited number of options, and preferably no more than five or six choices per category. The person thinking of the category (the sender) should write down the item chosen without the other person (the receiver) seeing this. Next the sender should concentrate on this item, while the other person mentally tries to pick this up and write it down. Do this a series of times with a number of items—ten makes a good number. Then, look at the number of "hits" (accurate guesses), and see if it's better than chance.

The higher the number of hits beyond chance, the more this suggests the possibility of ESP. (Incidentally, the way to determine chance is by the number of possibilities.) Divide the possibility of a hit (1) by that number. Thus, if there are five items, you have a one out of five chance of getting it right; if there are four items, you have a chance of winning one out of four; and so on. Turn this chance to a successful answer into a percentage (for instance, one right answer out of five chances will turn into 20 percent; one out of four chances gives you 25 percent). Finally, divide the number of hits in the series of guesses you just made (i.e., three right out of ten or 30 percent). If your percentage of hits is substantially greater than what you might have expected by chance, that's a sign of possible ESP.

After one person does a series of these, switch roles, or alternate thinking of items and guessing. Finally, compare your results to see which of you might have the highest ESP.

Notice the Differences on a Foreign Airline

Airlines have a certain personality or style that reflects their national culture to some extent. If you are on a foreign airline, try comparing the difference with airlines in the United States. Think about how these differences point to larger cultural differences.

Consider the differences in food, the way the stewards are dressed, type of service provided, the comments of the pilot or crew, seating arrangements, and so on. For example, if you are on a Japanese airline, you might notice the gracious service, attention to detail, and careful design used to present the food, all reflecting the Japanese concern with service and aesthetics. By contrast, when I was on an Aeroflot (Russian) flight, there seemed to be a no-frills, down-to-earth quality about the service. The food was plain and simple, the service was casual and minimal, and there were no differences in the class of the seating. All were designed to be equally simple and functional.

Make Your Waiting Time More Interesting

Much of traveling time is waiting—in airports, in hotel lobbies, in bus and train stations, to get through security checks, and worst, through customs if you travel abroad. This waiting time can often drag, particularly with extended delays. But there are numerous ways to make the time go faster and turn what might seem like wasted time into an enjoyable experience. Some of these techniques, which are just mentioned briefly, have been introduced as ways to make your ride or flight more interesting. In addition, some alternative techniques, described here, are especially useful when you are waiting.

Write Down Your Reflections and Impressions

Any extended waiting period can be an ideal time to review your impressions and experiences of the trip and write down your reflections, as previously described. Ideally, find an out-of-the-way place to do this, since you will face fewer distractions. If you are with others, ask someone to let you know when the group is ready to move on, so you don't have to keep jumping up to check on the schedule.

Use Your Camera

If you're a photo bug, waiting times can be a source of great shots, both where you are waiting or outside, if you have a half-hour or more and can leave the waiting area and wander around outside. You can explore nearby city streets, a market, station, or other areas. Even if you are waiting in a fairly modern airport, train station, or bus terminal, you may notice some unusual bits of local color, though check if it's okay to take photos where you are, due to national security concerns. It may be fine in the outer waiting area, but not once you go through the security checkpoint.

Should you enjoy taking photographs of people, waiting places can be ideal, because you've got a captive audience; many other people will be sitting around and waiting, too. Many waiting areas are also ideal because you can obtain a cross section of the population. For instance, at train stations and airports, people arrive from all over the country and often from other countries, and you can photograph a variety of people of different ethnicities to put together a broad profile of the place you have visited.

Your camera may also provide an excuse to explore the area and perhaps look into places where travelers don't normally go, such as behind the scenes at a nearby market. Just be sure to get permissions and comply with any applicable local rules and regulations. That's because some cities and countries are relatively loose about what people can do, while other countries can be quite strict. So make sure what you are doing is acceptable.

Ask a local official or your tour guide, if you have one, to make sure.

Where Are You Going Next? Plan Ahead!

Long waits are an excellent time to pull out your city or area guidebook calendar for where you are going next and read about the attractions. You will be better informed about what you will be visiting, and this prior knowledge may help you enjoy what you see even more. A review can help you decide on what to see; and even if you are on an organized tour, you can add in "must-see" places that aren't on the normal itinerary.

To plan in an organized way, have both a guide and a map of the place you are going. Besides store-bought fold-up maps, you can also get maps of most areas on www.mapquest.com or on Google Maps. You can zoom in or out on these online maps, so you can get both a bird's-eye view of the whole area and then zoom in and target a small section of blocks in a neighborhood. Check off the places you want to be sure to see, and star those that are especially important.

Next, take your map and locate these destinations. After you have plotted the destinations and how important they are to you, work out your itinerary to realistically cover as much of the most important activities and events as you can. This can be especially helpful if you are on a business trip and have limited time for sightseeing. This review can also help to decide if you want to skip any formal tours to get to the places you most want to see. But before you do, it's a good idea to check to be sure the places you want to see are open at the times you want to go, since schedules may change at the last minute and you don't want to end up going on your own to something that never gets going.

Take Some Time for Brainstorming

An especially profitable use of waiting time is brainstorming new ideas. Find a quiet place and use the time to come up with ideas for new projects, future plans, or a solution to a personal or business problem. If you are with a group in a waiting area, brainstorm something of group interest. For example, if you are traveling with business associates, you might try to solve a business problem related to your business. If you are traveling with friends, you might brainstorm ideas about where to go or what to do at your next destination. If you're with a tour group, come up with ideas for a party or celebration. Or take any topic to brainstorm just for fun and ask someone to pose a question for the whole group to react to, such as: "What are all the ways in which I can do . . ."

Arrange to coordinate the group brainstorming yourself or delegate this role to another person, or perhaps act as a co-coordinator with another person. If you don't already have a topic for brainstorming, invite others to suggest a topic. Everyone should throw out any suggestions they want as quickly as possible. All suggestions should be framed in a positive way, and the other participants should feel free to piggyback ideas onto previous suggestions, but they should not shoot an idea down. Also, the person being given suggestions should not respond with a "yes, but" to any suggestion. Rather, he should listen to everyone else's ideas, and as appropriate, add his own ideas.

While this process is going on, at least one person should write down the suggestions on a sheet of paper, laptop, or on a whiteboard in front of the group. After everyone has finished coming up with suggestions, the person asking the questions or members of the whole group can evaluate these ideas to decide which ones to put into practice. Then, the person asking the questions should rate the suggestions according to which ones he or she likes best. Later, he or she can put the highest priority ideas into practice, if they are deemed good enough. If the responses are for a group question, the members of the group should vote and decide their priorities as a group.

By using this process, you will not only make your waiting time more interesting, but you may come up with some profitable and productive ideas, too.

Getting to Know Other People

Waiting time is also good for getting to know others who are waiting and looking for something to do. This can be especially enjoyable if you are traveling with co-workers who you don't know very well. What better time to get to know someone than sitting in an airport terminal? You may find that you have a lot in common and you may develop a work friendship with somebody you barely knew.

But this approach can be fun with people you've never seen before, too. If you are sitting or standing in line next to someone who looks interesting, you can start by making a few brief comments to break the ice. If the person seems receptive, continue the conversation.

Some possible openers are:

- Making an observation about your present situation, though be sure to keep your comments upbeat and positive, so it doesn't sound like you are complaining. You also want to open up the conversation for a further response, with a statement such as: "All this security reminds me of the school where I teach."

- Another possible opener might be to comment on something about the person that seems interesting or attractive, or to remark on anything that you have in common. For example, if the person is wearing an interesting pin or necklace, mention this. Or if you are both sitting with luggage and you notice from the tag that this person comes from your home state, note your common background.

Once you've gotten the conversation going, you might ask about his or her background, travel plans, experiences on the trip, opinions, etc. You'll find that people who are waiting around will often be very receptive to an extended conversation, since, like you, they may be impatient with waiting and eager to find interesting stimulation. If you sense the person indicates by her brief or hesitant answers that she doesn't feel like talking, politely ease off. If you want to close off the conversation yourself, you might mention you have other things to do or politely excuse yourself, move to another part of the waiting area, and talk to someone else.

Tuning In to the People You See

Another way to pass time enjoyably while waiting is to pay more attention to the people around you and really "tune in" to them. The process can be like watching a movie or play or you might experience projecting your imagination into someone else and looking at the world from their point of view.

You can use this technique anywhere—in a station, on the street, in line in a store—and with anyone. It's an especially good technique to use in a foreign country, where you don't know the language and can't speak to most of the people around you. Instead of talking, obtain a sense of the culture by tuning in this way.

One technique is to imagine that everyone is moving past you on a movie screen or stage, so that you feel a sense of detachment. Observe, and ask yourself questions. Notice what people are wearing; watch where they are going. Pay attention to the subtleties of the way people interact together, how far apart they stand, how fast they walk. And notice any cultural differences. For example, people in the United States tend to stand much farther apart than people in Mexico; New Yorkers walk much faster than people in London or Paris. The more you experiment with looking, the more differences you will observe.

You'll notice differences in how people look and what they are wearing, too, as you travel from city to city within the same country or in different parts of the same city. In waiting areas, you may be in an excellent position to observe such differences, because you are in a place where a cross section of the local community passes by.

Another approach is to project your consciousness into the people you see and imagine that you are that person for a moment. Then, as that person, try to experience what he or she is seeing or feeling. For example, if a stylishly dressed woman walks by, imagine you are that woman, and what she may be thinking or feeling. If she stops to talk to someone, imagine what she might be saying and how she might be feeling about the person she's talking to. Or, as she walks around, imagine how she sees the world around her and how she feels about herself and the people who pass by.

It's always harder to see the world from someone else's point of view. But as you practice, you'll grow better at it, and you'll find this technique will help give you a real sense of other people and cultures. It's like stepping into the shoes of other people for a closer, more personal look.

Taking Time Out to Meditate

An extended period of waiting can also be excellent for meditation or for focusing inward. Meditating may help you relax. If you are starting to feel anxious or impatient because of the wait, meditation may soothe these feelings. If you are familiar with some meditative practice, you can use that or you can use the technique described below.

To meditate most effectively, find a fairly quiet, out-of-the-way place where you can feel comfortable closing your eyes for a while. Since many people take catnaps in waiting rooms, this can be a good place to use. It's best to assume an upright sitting position with your feet planted firmly on the floor. Close your eyes and concentrate on your breathing for a minute or two to calm down. Notice your breath going in and out, in and out, in and out . . .

When you achieve a calm, relaxed state, think of a simple word or sound (i.e., the word "one," "om," etc.), and concentrate on that word. Seek to let your mind go blank. If other thoughts pass through your mind, simply acknowledge them and let them go. Ignore any surrounding sounds; similarly acknowledge them and let go. Then return to focus on your word or sound.

Do this for fifteen to thirty minutes. You can use a watch or traveling alarm clock, or if you are with a group, ask someone to let you know when time is up. Alternatively, simply continue the exercise for as long as you want until you feel really relaxed.

Experimenting with Being Aware

Another enjoyable, relaxing activity while waiting is to experiment with being aware. Concentrate on what you are experiencing with senses you don't normally use.

What do I mean? For example, you might start by closing your eyes and relaxing, as if you were going to meditate. Choose a comfortable place, where you can close your eyes without feeling overly conspicuous. However, instead of focusing within and trying to keep your mind blank, pay careful attention to everything around you.

Once you feel relaxed, notice what the environment is like

around you. Be aware of sounds, and notice where they are coming from. Are they close? Far away? Who or what might be making them? Is the sound loud? Soft? What is the texture or tone of the sound?

If you hear voices, listen. Notice how you can move your attention from one set of voices or sounds to another. Imagine that the sounds form an amphitheater around you, and experience yourself surrounded by sound.

Pay attention to any smells. Don't worry if you can't identify them immediately. Instead, simply focus on the smells. Notice where they are coming from. Be aware of how two or more smells may blend together. If you can, think of yourself in a landscape of smells, and notice what you experience.

Be aware of your sense of touch. Pay attention to any vibrations you feel against your body, any movements under your feet. Notice the temperature around you.

Look within and notice how you are feeling now. Are you comfortable? Relaxed? Calm? Powerful? Confident? Peaceful? You may experience a number of feelings at the same time.

Finally, tell yourself, "I'm feeling really good. I'm feeling very comfortable, calm, and relaxed," and notice that you now feel this way. Savor this feeling for a minute or two. When you are finished, open your eyes—you may be surprised at how really good you feel.

14

Start an *ENJOY!* Group to Increase Your Fun with Others

The previous chapters have focused on ways to increase your enjoyment with techniques you use on your own or by taking the initiative in suggesting activities for your co-workers or team members to do at work. But beyond these activities, you can join with others in a more systematic way to apply these techniques. This way you both have a support group and a group to help you continually come up with creative and fun ideas to add more enjoyment to everyone's life.

Think of this group as a Master Mind Alliance, brainstorming group, and buddy system all rolled into one. In fact, you can use it as a kind of "fun ideas" incubator to try out new ideas before you begin using them yourself on a regular basis or introducing them to others in your workplace. The group can also be a way of jointly trying out suggested techniques in the book, going through the book on a chapter-by-chapter basis, or selecting chapters in an order voted on by the group.

Creating an *ENJOY!* Group

If there isn't already an *ENJOY!* Group in your area, create one. Some ideal candidates for this might be people you meet in various activities you participate in to add more enjoyment in your life or co-workers who you feel especially close to and would like to participate in activities with off the job.

A good way to start a group is to think through what you want the group to do over the first few months, so you have an initial program in place. This way, the first people to come to the group will quickly see the potential and determine if this is a group they want to belong to. You don't want to turn the first meeting into a general discussion about using the group to promote ways to add enjoyment to your lives. That's no fun and the meeting can quickly become academic and theoretical—which for most people isn't much fun.

Instead, start with something that's fun and save the discussion about what the group is going to do and who is going to do what until the end of the meeting, say the last twenty or thirty minutes. To this end, work up an agenda for the program and pick out a mix of techniques that you think the people you invite will enjoy. Then, invite people personally or write up a short flyer to give to people at work and in your personal and social network. Figure on a group of between six and ten people, so you keep it small and casual, which is good for a group featuring sharing, support, and experiential techniques.

Plan on about three hours for an initial meeting—say from about 7–10 P.M. (You can always end early.) If you want to start with a potluck, add in an additional half-hour in the beginning for the food and socializing. Figure on an agenda that might be structured something like this:

7:00–7:15—Arrivals and initial socializing
7:15–7:30—Introductions and statements about what people hope to get out of the group

7:30–9:00—Introduce selected techniques and exercises for the group, or pick a chapter and introduce some exercises from that. These exercises might include visualizations, games, shared dreaming about fun things to do, etc. After each exercise, invite some feedback and discussion, so you know what works well and what doesn't, and you or others putting on meetings can use this for helpful future planning. You might also invite people to share on their especially enjoyable experiences during the past day or week.

9:00–9:30—Discuss what people think about the group and where they would like to see it go. Invite people to engage in initial planning, such as suggesting and selecting programs for the future, and seek volunteers to lead group activities or host meetings in their homes. Ask people for preferred meeting dates and times, and if possible, set a future date or if people are unsure of their schedules, invite feedback by e-mail and suggest a few alternate times, so you can find out the preferred date and time, and schedule future meetings accordingly. Ask how often people want to meet (i.e., weekly, biweekly, monthly) and if people would like to keep meeting in the same place (i.e., your house) or would like to rotate hosting the group.

9:30–10—Additional socializing and goodbyes.

While it might be convenient for you to keep the meetings at your house, it can help others feel more invested in the group if you have a rotating meeting place and pass on leadership for each meeting to the person hosting the meeting. This way the group feels more democratic and involving. However, in the beginning while you are nurturing this idea, you might initially organize and host the meetings.

It is also helpful to have more frequent meetings—say once a week or twice a month—if you want to make this more of a support-and-brainstorming group. This way, people can regularly work on different exercises and report on their progress. If people have overly busy schedules, set up the meetings for once a month. Then, as the group gathers steam, seek to meet more often and draw in people who can make a greater time commitment.

You might also suggest that the attendees who are ready to commit to coming to the group on a regular basis team up to create *ENJOY!* Buddies—partners with whom they can share ideas they come up with during the week, discuss anything interfering with their ability to experience more enjoyment, and so forth.

Choosing Initial Activities for the Meeting

Figure on about an hour and a half for activities and sharing, and vary the types of activities you present. A good way to start is to introduce *ENJOY!*, which you will be using as a guide in setting up the group. Describe the different areas of increasing enjoyment featured in the book, perhaps by going through the table of contents and briefly noting what each chapter is about. (The Introduction can guide you through this.) Then, depending on the group, pick a chapter to start with or select some of your favorite exercises and techniques from the book.

It's also good to vary the type of activities. For instance, you might start with some initial sharing about the most enjoyable experiences people had during the last few days or weeks and why, followed by a brief discussion about how other people have had similar enjoyable experiences. Then, you might invite people to share something they experienced that they didn't like and what they would change to make it better in the future.

Next, you might try out various exercises. You can pick a chapter in the book that especially appeals to you and group members, go through the book in sequence with the group, or choose specific techniques you like. It's good to mix up the type of exercises you use to vary the experience, say combining a visualization exercise with a game or physical exercise. However, feel free to focus on one type of exercise if group members prefer this.

After each exercise, take some time for everyone to talk about their experience. Notice what people especially like, so you can emphasize those types of exercises in the future, or don't like, so you know which exercises to stop using.

Suggest that people keep a journal or notebook devoted to both their personal experiences in learning to enjoy their life and work more and on their experiences in the group. This can also be a place to keep notes on the group meetings, so they can refer to these notes and use these for further insights.

If desired, you can also incorporate photos or video clips into the program, such as if people want to show photos or videos to illustrate an especially enjoyable experience. Invite people to pass around prints, or if you have a laptop, desktop computer, or DVD player set up, you can show JPEGs or play audio or video files. But keep these clips short—no more than two or three minutes, since you don't want the focus to be on viewing or listening to someone doing or saying something.

While it's good to have an overall agenda for the meeting, you should be ready to vary it, based on what group members would prefer to do. After all, this is a group devoted to enjoying work and life more, so keep the meeting fun and enjoyable, too.

Planning for Future Activities and Meeting Dates

At the end of your first meeting, devote about a half-hour to planning future meetings—what the program will be, who will be hosting the meetings, where they will be, when and how often they will occur. Then, at future meetings, once the logistics are arranged, you can cover this future planning in a few minutes.

Initially, it's important to clarify the purpose of the group and get the participants' ideas for future meetings, so you get the buy-in for those who want to continue attending group meetings. Then, once the group has a clear sense of its purpose and you know who wants to continue to attend, schedule the next meeting, and decide where and when it will be. If anyone is unsure, follow up with e-mail to determine if they will be coming to the next meeting or not, and if they will be attending any meetings in the future.

Get everyone's e-mail addresses, too, and share these with other participants. Send everyone an e-mail about how much you enjoyed having them at the meeting and confirming when the next meeting will be. Later, whoever is hosting the next meeting might take over the responsibility of notifying and reminding everyone by e-mail about the next meeting.

Winding Up the Meeting

Devote the last part of the meeting to informal socializing and snacking. If you started with a potluck, you can simply resume this, or simply bring out snacks and beverages at this time.

Most of all, have fun! Make sure to enjoy yourself and help all the other members of the group enjoy themselves, too. That's the whole idea of getting together!

PART V

Putting It All Together

15

The Enjoyment Assessment Quiz

So there you have it—an overall guide to putting more fun in your work—and in your life as well. Let's quickly recap the four key ideas presented in this book:

1. The first step is to *improve your attitude*, so you feel more upbeat and happy in general. By understanding the secrets of being happy, such as showing appreciation, building on your strengths, and using positive language, you can bring that outlook into the workplace. And that will not only help you feel more cheerful, but it will inspire others to feel better about being and working with you.

2. You also need to *overcome any personal barriers to enjoyment*, such as quieting your inner critical voice and being able to let out your inner kid, so you feel free to let go and enjoy. It also helps to assess where you are now, as well as keep an enjoyment journal to chart your progress.

3. The core concept of this book is to *learn to enjoy your work*. One key to enjoying your work now is finding ways to make even routine work more interesting. That way, whether you

want to do the work or not, it becomes more fun. Plus, there are all sorts of ways to liven up your workplace with others. While management often takes the lead in introducing fun workplace activities to increase morale, teamwork, and productivity, such as dress-up days and holiday celebrations, you can take the initiative in many cases to introduce ideas to your co-workers and plan activities and events.

4. Finally, there are all kinds of ways to *expand your fun horizons* on and off the job, such as trying new activities and events you have never done before and applying assorted awareness, perception, and enjoyment techniques to enhance everyday activities. Still other techniques can help you find fun things to do on downtime, such as when you are driving or flying somewhere, or simply waiting for something to happen.

This book has provided a compendium of techniques you can use, whether you read the book straight through from chapter to chapter or dip around to pick out the chapters and techniques that most interest you.

Taking the Enjoyment Assessment Quiz

So how high is your own Enjoyment Quotient? Here's a short quiz you can take now to show you how you rate. Then try again later, after you have had some time to practice some of these techniques, and your Enjoyment Quotient should increase even more.

The 25 questions are based on the major topics covered in *ENJOY! 101 Little Ways to Add Fun to Your Work Every Day*. Rate how well you think you do in each area; then total your score.

To determine your score, answer the following questions honestly, and answer every question. If you aren't sure, it is usually best to go with your initial response.

The higher your score, the more you enjoy your work and your workplace, as well as other things in your life (since there is a high correlation between enjoying your work and what's happening in your life).

Here's the quiz. Rate yourself from 0 to 5 on each question, then add up the totals. See the scoring key at the end to see how well you have done.

Your Attitude

_____ 1. I usually have an upbeat, cheerful, positive attitude.

_____ 2. I am normally optimistic that things will go well.

_____ 3. I like to be proactive and take the initiative to get things I want to get.

_____ 4. I usually feel very secure and confident about myself and what I do.

_____ 5. I like being altruistic and helping others.

_____ 6. I appreciate myself and I don't let the criticisms of others get to me.

_____ 7. I feel I have made the right career choice for me.

Your Ability to Overcome Any Barriers to Enjoyment

_____ 8. I don't feel I have any barriers to enjoyment.

_____ 9. I don't have an inner critical voice that keeps me from doing what I want to do.

_____ 10. I feel I am in touch with my inner kid.

_____ 11. I feel comfortable relaxing and letting go.

_____ 12. I can easily use my imagination and powers of visualization.

_____ 13. I don't have many worries.

Your Level of Fun at Work

_____ 14. I really like the work I am doing now.

_____ 15. I really like the people I am working with.

_____ 16. Even when my work is routine, I find ways to make it interesting.

_____ 17. I have created an attractive, enjoyable workspace around me.

_____ 18. I do fun things during lunch or work breaks.

_____ 19. Our workplace has fun activities, events, and celebrations.

Your Fun Horizons On and Off the Job

_____ 20. I enjoy trying out new activities and events.

_____ 21. I'm involved in a wide variety of fun activities off the job.

_____ 22. I have an active imagination I can use in imagining a variety of fun activities.

_____ 23. I don't often get bored.

_____ 24. I can easily find ways to amuse myself, no matter what I am doing.

_____ 25. I'm good at brainstorming and coming up with new ideas for things to do on and off the job.

_____ TOTAL SCORE

The Rating System

Think of this like a "Fun-O-Meter" that you use to rate how much you enjoy or are having fun at work. It's a guide to how well you are doing now. Then, use the results to help you increase your "Enjoyment Quotient" score by improving where you are weak, so you have even more fun.

90 + = You are definitely a lot of fun and great to work with. Have you considered the comedy stand-up circuit?

80–89 = You are usually full of fun and a fun person to be around. Keep up the good cheer.

70–79 = You may encounter some bumps along the way to having fun, but you can usually turn things around, so things are mostly fun.

60–69 = Uh-oh. Things are sometimes not so good. Consider ways to improve your ability to have fun.

40–59 = You've got to find some ways to bring more fun into your life. You need a fun fix now, before things get any worse.

0–39 = Your FUNdamentals are way off. You need to quickly add some fun to your life and add some good FUNdations, or watch out. Your FUN house is on its way to an early collapse.

Notes

Chapter 1

1. Dan Baker and Cameron Stauth, *What Happy People Know* (New York: St. Martin's Griffin, 2004), p. 5.
2. Ibid., p. 7.
3. Ibid., p. 10.
3. Ibid., p. 12.
4. Ibid., pp. 19–21.
5. Ibid., p. 19.

Chapter 2

1. Baker and Stauth, pp. 37–78.
2. Ibid., pp. 37–40.
3. Ibid., p. 37.
4. Ibid., p. 81.
5. Ibid., pp. 95–96.
6. Ibid., pp. 96–97.
7. Ibid, pp. 129–131.
8. Ibid., p. 115.
9. Ibid., pp. 121–122.
10. Ibid., p. 123.
11. Ibid, p. 135, citing Tara Bennett-Goldeman in *Emotional Alchemy.*
12. Ibid., p. 145.
13. Ibid., pp. 148, 153.

14. Ibid., pp. 183–184.
15. Ibid., p. 184.
16. Ibid., pp. 216–217.
17. Ibid., p. 226.
18. Ibid., p. 62.
19. Ibid., p. 73.

Chapter 3

1. David Niven, *100 Simple Secrets of Happy People: What Scientists Have Learned and How You Can Use It* (San Francisco: HarperSanFrancisco, 2006), p. xvii.
2. A. Al-Amri and M. Lee, "The Relationship between Job Satisfaction and Life Satisfaction," *Journal of the Social Sciences,* 24:289, 1996.
3. Michael Argyle, Maryanne Martin, and Luo Lu, "Testing for Stress and Happiness: The Role of Social and Cognitive Factors," in *Stress and Emotion* (Washington, D.C.: Taylor & Francis, 1995).
4. E. Change and A. Maydeu-Olivares, "Optimism and Pessimism and Partially Independent Constructs: Relationship to Positive and Negative Affectivity and Psychological Well-Being," *Personality and Individual Differences* 23:433, 1997.
5. Niven, p. 17.
6. Niven, p. 9.
7. Niven, p. 21, citing a study by C. Murray and M. J. Peacock: "A Model-Free Approach to the Study of Subjective Well-Being, in *Mental Health in Black America* (Thousand Oaks, Calif.: Sage, 1996).
8. Niven, p. 26.
9. E. Diener and F. Fujita, "Resources, Personal Strivings, and Subjective Well-Being," *Journal of Personality and Social Psychology,* 68:926, 1995, cited by Niven, p. 50.

Chapter 5

1. Michael Ray and Rochelle Myers, *Creativity in Business* (Garden City, N.Y.: Doubleday & Company, 1986), pp. 39–40.
2. Ibid., p. 42.
3. Ibid., p. 43.
4. Ibid., p. 44.

5. Ibid., p. 45.
6. Ibid., p. 59.
7. Ibid., pp. 49–50.
8. Ibid., p. 51.
9. Ibid., p. 53.
10. Ibid., p. 53.
11. Ibid., pp. 62–63.

Chapter 6

1. Johan Huizinga, *Homo Ludens: A Study of the Play Element in Culture* (New York: Harper & Row, 1970), p. 22.
2. Ibid., p. 27.
3. Gini Graham Scott, *Mind Power* (Upper Saddle River, N.J.: Prentice Hall, 1989), pp. 163–175.
4. Gini Graham Scott, *Fantasy Worlds* (Lincoln, Nebr.: ASJA Press, 2006), pp. 201–212.

Chapter 8

1. Dave Hemsath and Leslie Yerkes, *301 Ways to Have Fun at Work* (San Francisco: Berrkett-Koehler, 1997), pp. 6–7.
2. Ibid., p. 16.
3. Ibid., p. 59.
4. Joy Sikorski, *How to Draw a Radish* (San Francisco: Chronicle Books, 1995).
5. Ibid., p. 7.
6. Ibid., pp. 9–33.
7. Ibid., pp. 47–79.
8. Ibid., pp. 36–38.
9. Ibid., p. 101.
10. Ibid., p. 117.
11. Ibid., p. 120.
12. Ibid., pp. 136–137.
13. Ibid., p. 139.
14. Ibid., p. 147.
15. Ibid., pp. 156–157.
16. Ibid., p. 187.
17. Hemsath and Yerkes, pp. 63–64.

Chapter 9

1. Hemsath and Yerkes, pp. 23–24.
2. Ibid., p. 29.
3. Ibid., pp. 214–215.
4. Ibid., p. 102.
5. Ibid., p. 210.
6. Dave Hemsath, *301 More Ways to Have Fun at Work* (San Francisco: Berrett-Koehler, 2001), pp. 155–156.

Chapter 10

1. Hemsath and Yerkes, p. 15.
2. Ibid., p. 178.
3. www.larrywilde.com/month.htm.
4. Hemsath and Yerkes, p. 142.
5. Hemsath, pp. 57–58.
6. Ibid, p. 89.
7. Ibid., p. 151.

Chapter 11

1. Hemsath and Yerkes, p. 209.

Chapter 12

1. Joint Center for Housing Studies, October 6, 2006, p. 11.

Chapter 13

1. Gini Graham Scott, *The Creative Traveler* (Lincoln, Nebr.: ASJA Press, 2007).

Selected Bibliography

Following are some books on enjoying your work or life more or on making the workplace more fun. I have drawn on some of them in writing this book.

Books on Enjoying Work More

Adams, Scott. *The Joy of Work: Dilbert's Guide to Finding Happiness at the Expense of Your Co-Workers.* New York: HarperBusiness, 1999.

Bakke, Dennis W. *Joy at Work: A Revolutionary Approach to Fun on the Job.* Seattle, Wash.: PVG, 2005. Deals with changing the work environment in a particular company and is directed toward CEOs and top executives.

Boyadjian, Berge. *Create Fun @ Work: Improve Your Productivity, Quality of Life, and the Morale of Those Around You.* Long Beach, Calif.: Knowledge Capture and Transfer, 1999.

Erickson, Melinda Howard. *How to Work Smart! And Enjoy Your Job: 25 Simple Ways to Be Recognized, Appreciated, Respected, and Valued.* Seattle, Wash.: Kingston Press, 2002.

Hemsath, Dave. *301 More Ways to Have Fun at Work.* San Francisco: Berrett-Koehler, 2001.

Hemsath, Dave, and Leslie Yerkes. *301 Ways to Have Fun at Work*. San Francisco: Berrett-Koehler, 1997.

Livingston, William. *Have Fun at Work*. New York: F.E.S. Ltd. Publishing, 1990.

Sikorski, Joy. *How to Draw a Radish: and Other Fun Things to do at Work*. San Francisco: Chronicle Books, 1995.

Veeck, Mike, and Pete Williams. *Fun Is Good: How to Create Joy and Passion in Your Workplace and Career*. Emmaus, Pa.: Rodale, 2005.

Books on Finding Happiness

Baker, Dan, and Cameron Stauth. *What Happy People Know: How the New Science of Happiness Can Change Your Life for the Better*. New York: St. Martin's Griffin, 2003.

Carnegie, Dale. *How to Enjoy Your Life and Your Job*. New York: Pocket, 1990.

The Dalai Lama and Howard C. Cutler. *The Art of Happiness: A Handbook for Living*. New York: Penguin Putnam, 1998.

The Dalai Lama and Howard C. Cutler. *The Art of Happiness at Work*. London: Riverhead Books, 2003.

McGowan, Todd. *The End of Dissatisfaction: Jacques Lacan and the Emerging Society of Enjoyment*. Albany: State University of New York Press, 2003. Academic study of society focused around enjoyment.

Niven, David. *The 100 Simple Secrets of Happy People: What Scientists Have Learned and How You Can Use It*. New York: HarperSanFrancisco, 2000.

Ryan, Mary Jane. *The Happiness Makeover: How to Teach Yourself to Be Happy and Enjoy Every Day*. New York: Broadway Books, 2005.

Salmansohn, Karen, and Don Zinzell. *How to Be Happy, Dammit: A Cynic's Guide to Spiritual Happiness*. Berkeley, Calif.: Celestial Arts, 2001.

Books on Slowing Down or Simplifying to Enjoy Your Life More

Molloy, Andrea. *Stop Living Your Job Start Living Your Life: 85 Simple Strategies to Achieve Work/Life Balance*. Berkeley, Calif.: Ulysses Press, 2005.

Ryan, Mary Jane. *The Power of Patience: How to Slow the Rush and Enjoy More Happiness, Success, and Peace of Mind Everyday*. New York: Broadway Books, 2003.

Salmansohn, Karen. *How to Change Your Entire Life by Doing Absolutely Nothing: 10 Do-Nothing Relaxation Exercises to Calm You Down Quickly So You Can Speed Forward Faster*. New York: Simon & Schuster, 2003.

St. James, Elaine. *Simplify Your Life: 100 Ways to Slow Down and Enjoy the Things that Really Matter*. New York: Hyperion, 1994.

St. James, Elaine. *Simplify Your Work Life: Ways to Change So You Have More Time to Live*. New York: Hyperion, 2001.

Books of Positive Quotes and Affirmations

Eldershaw, Jane. *The Little Book of Moods: 101 Ways to Embrace and Enjoy Any Emotion*. Cincinnati, Ohio: Adams Media Corporation, 2004.

Klein, Allen. *The Wise and Witty Quote Book: 2000 Quotations to Enlighten, Encourage, and Enjoy*. New York: Gramercy Publishing, 2005.

Salmansohn, Karen. *Quickie Stickies: 100 Pick-Me-Ups for When You're Feeling Unglued*. New York: Workman Publishing, 2003.

Finding Happiness by Looking Within

Gallwey, W. Timothy. *The Inner Game of Work*. New York: Random House, 2000.

Lightman, Dana. *POWER Optimism: Enjoy the Life You Have . . . Create the Success You Want*. Abington, Pa.: POWER Optimism, 2004.

Mohr, Matthew D. *Glad to Be Living Life: Creating More Enjoyment in Your Life*. Fargo, N.D.: Dacotah Paper Company, 2003.

Weiler, Nicholas W., and Stephen C. Schoonover. *Your Soul at Work: Five Steps to a More Fulfilling Career and Life*. Mahwah, N.J.: Hidden-Spring, 2001.

Finding Your Calling or Life's Work

Jensen, Bill. *What is Your Life's Work?* New York: HarperBusiness, 2005.

Leider, Richard J. *The Power of Purpose: Creating Meaning in Your Life and Work*. San Francisco: Berrett-Koehler, 2004.

Leider, Richard J., and David A. Shapiro. *Whistle While You Work: Healing Your Life's Calling.* San Francisco: Berrett-Koehler, 2001.

Books for Managers on Creating a More Enjoyable Workplace

Weinstein, Matt. *Dogs Don't Bite When a Growl Will Do.* New York: Perigee/Penguin Books, 2003.

Weinstein, Matt. *Managing to Have Fun.* New York: Simon & Schuster, 1997.

Weinstein, Matt. *Work Like Your Dog.* New York: Villard Books, Random House, 1999.

Proving Rewards and Recognition

Aguanno, Kevin. *101 Ways to Reward Team Members for $20 (or Less).* Lakeland, Ontario: Multi-Media Publications, 2003.

Gostick, Adrian, and Chester Elton. *A Carrot a Day: A Daily Dose of Recognition for Your Employees.* Salt Lake City: Gibbs Smith, 2004.

Gostick, Adrian, and Chester Elton. *The Carrot Principle.* New York: Free Press, 2007.

Gostick, Adrian, and Chester Elton. *Managing with Carrots: Using Recognition to Attract and Retain the Best People.* Salt Lake City: Gibbs Smith, 2001.

Gostick, Adrian, and Chester Elton. *The 24-Carrot Manager: A Remarkable Story of How a Leader Can Unleash Human Potential.* Salt Lake City: Gibbs Smith, 2002.

Nelson, Bob. *1001 Ways to Energize Employees.* New York: Workman Publishing, 1997.

Ventrice, Cindy. *Make Their Day: Employee Recognition That Works, Simple Ways to Boost Morale, Productivity, and Profits.* San Francisco: Berrett-Koehler, 2003.

Games for Promoting Teamwork and Other Work Activities

Caroselli, Marlene. *Productive Meetings*. New York: McGraw-Hill, 2002.

Epstein, Robert, and Jessica Rogers. *The Big Book of Motivation Games: Quick Fun Activities for Energizing People at Work and at Home*. New York: McGraw-Hill, 2001.

Newstrom, John, and Edward Scannell. *The Big Book of Team Building Games: Trust-Building Activities, Team Spirit Exercises, and Other Fun Things to Do*. New York: McGraw-Hill, 1998.

Newstrom, John, and Edward Scannell. *The Big Book of Business Games: Icebreakers, Creativity Exercises, and Meeting Energizers*. New York: McGraw-Hill, 1996.

Tamblyn, Doni, and Sharyn Weiss. *The Big Book of Humorous Training Games*. New York: McGraw-Hill, 2000.

Index

rewards-and-recognition party,
156–157
riddles, posting, 122
rides, fun during, 187–193
by asking tour guide questions,
192–193
by imagining yourself in the setting, 187–188
by photographing while you ride,
190–191
with "seeing" games, 188
by taking time to write, 190
with travel bingo, 188–190
by turning stops into miniadven-
tures, 191–192
Roosevelt, Theodore, 24
routine work
finding fun in, 49
music during, 130
perking up, 111–113

Safeway, 130
sales parties, 174
Sapir-Whorf hypothesis, 28
satisfaction, sources of, 39
"Say It" contest, 139–140
scavenger hunts, 151
schedule, work, 46–47
Scream Teams, 135
second-life experiences, 182–183
Secret Santa gift exchange, 146,
162–163
security, feelings of
as quality of happiness, 5
reaffirming, 8
seeing games, 188
self-judgment, 70
self-talk, 117
services, creative new ideas for, 161
setbacks, 40
settings, imagining yourself in,
187–188

share-the-wealth reward tradition,
160
showing appreciation, 13–17
Showtime, 140
Sikorski, Joy, 125, 126
Simonds, Laura, 161–162
singing while you work, 118
Skinner, B. F., 35
smiling, 44
social connection services, 180
songs
about work, 165–166
in your head, 115
sources of happiness, 39, 55, 57–58
sources of joy/fun, 57–58
space travel fantasy, 90–93
spirituality
in difficult circumstances, 8
as quality of happiness, 5
status symbols, 48
stories
increasing happiness by use of,
30–31
inspiring, 143
of vacations, 143
strengths, tapping into, 24–28
stress
learned helpless state of, 18–19
overcoming feelings of, 100–101
when not acting from personal
power, 22
stretch breaks, 114
success, measuring, 48
success tapes, sharing, 141
support
for others, 46
from others, 45
surprise parties, 162
survival game, 153–154

theme parties, 164, 168
thoughts